HURRAY GOD!

HOPEPRAYBELIEVE

COMPILED BY JEANETTE SHARP

WinePressPublishing
Great Books, Defined.

WinePress Publishing (PO Box 428, Enumclaw, WA 98022) functions only as book publisher. As such, the ultimate design, content, editorial accuracy, and views expressed or implied in this work are those of the author.

ISBN 13: 978-1-4141-1982-3
ISBN 10: 1-4141-1982-8
Library of Congress Catalog Card Number: 2010940429

HURRAY
GOD !

CONTENTS

Acknowledgments ix

Introduction. xi

Chapter 1: Work Is Good for the Soul 1
  In God's Time—*Linda O'Connell* 1
  Finding Gold—*Jeanette Sharp* 5
  Best Friends—*Janetta Messmer*. 9
  A Match Made in Heaven—*Sherri Langton* 12
  Show Me, Lord—*Elsa Dotson*. 15
  Success—Just a Prayer Away—*Susan Sundwall*. 19
  Prayer Confirmation—*Charlotte Holt* 22
  Prayer Nugget 25

Chapter 2: No Worries. 27
  The Collision—*Andrew Culbertson* 27
  Surrounded by Darkness—*Danielle VanMeter* 30
  A Sudden Slip—*Renie Burghardt* 32
  My Drowning Moment—*Sally Hanan*. 36
  Faith Under Fire—*Sally Clark* 38
  Mysterious Rescue—*Ann Denton as told to Esther M. Bailey*. 40
  Comfort for a Grandmother's Heart—*Grace Booth* 42
  Prayer Nugget 44

Chapter 3: Hey! I've Known You Forever 47
  Extraordinary Miracles; Everyday Faith—*Rebecca Joie Oakes* 47
  The Blessing of My Infertility—*Susan Kimmel Wright* 50
  Waiting for Our Miracle—*Perry Perkins*. 54
  The Mysterious Blonde—*Jeanette Sharp*. 56
  Fashionably Maternal—*Connie Alexander Huddleston* 60
  God Cares About the Smallest Details—*Carolyn R. Scheidies* 62
  Mom, I'm Losing Her!—*Aggie Stevenson* 64
  Prayer Nugget 68

Chapter 4: It's All in the Family 71
  At the End of the Fence—*Jan Cline, as told by my husband, Jerry* 71
  Department Store Angel—*Marilyn E. Freeman* 75
  The Faded, Brown-Leather Purse—*Debra Elliott* 78
  Restored Relationship—*Esther M. Bailey* 80
  From Praise to Paradise—*Sue Tornai* 83
  Prayer Nugget 85

Chapter 5: Gifts That Keep on Giving 87
  Close Encounters—*Mimi Greenwood Knight* 87
  And There Was Music in the Air—*Susan Kimmel Wright* 91
  Twins and Talent—*Kandy Sharp* 94
  Safe and Dry—*Lisa Keck* 96
  God-Incidence—*Lisa Plowman Dolensky* 98
  Prayer Nugget 102

Chapter 6: You'll Never Guess What Happened! 105
  The God Who Sees—*Denise Chang*. 105
  A Divine Appointment—*Twilah A. Fox, M.D.* 109
  The Perfect Storm—Our Perfect God—*Annette O'Hare* 111
  Shanghai Encounter—*Peggy Park*. 113
  Angels in Overalls—*Catherine Leggitt* 117
  My Stolen Bible—*Mike Lynch* 121
  Five Boxes of Christmas Cards—*Jeanette Sharp* 124
  Prayer Nugget 126

Chapter 7: Love Is Patient 129
　　The List—*Dwan Reed* 129
　　Just One Friend—*Peter Pollock*. 133
　　A Dream Is a Wish Your Heart Makes—*Marlayne Giron* 136
　　The Unanswered Letters—*Sherrie Murphree* 139
　　Why Doesn't He Answer?—*Yulia Bagwell* 141
　　Prayer Nugget 143

Chapter 8: Relax! I've Got It Covered. 145
　　A House in "Almost Heaven"—*Susan Carlton* 145
　　A Nest of Opportunities—*Terri Tiffany*. 148
　　Handled with Care—*Sheila Wipperman*. 152
　　The White, Baby Grand Piano—*Kandy Sharp*. 154
　　God's Provision for a Russian Girl—*Peggy Park*. 156
　　Prayer Nugget 158

Chapter 9: Is There Anything I Can't Do? 161
　　Chemical Crash—*Cindy Rooy* 161
　　Road Trip to Healing—*Carolyn R. Scheides* 164
　　Miracles Still Happen—*Leon Arceneaux*. 167
　　Nothing Is Too Small—*Lynn McCallum* 169
　　The Course That Almost Conquered Me—*Angela Banks*. 171
　　My Kung Fu Battle—*Steve Husting* 173
　　Prayer Nugget 175

Chapter 10: From A to Z. 177
　　Ordered Steps—*Anita Onarecker*. 177
　　The Prayer That Changed My Prayers—*Marty Prudhomme*. 179
　　Life Vigil—*Diana Amadeo*. 181
　　New Steps of Faith—*Vanessa Ingold*. 185
　　Flat Tires—*Barbara Russell Robinson* 187
　　Our Son Is Missing—*Robyn Cederstrand* 189
　　My Struggle with Cigarettes—*Edward Reinagel* 192
　　Not Guilty—*Natalie White* 194
　　Prayer Nugget 196

About the Contributors 199

Scripture List 207

ACKNOWLEDGMENTS

MANY THANKS . . .

To my precious Lord Jesus, Who planted the seed for this book in my heart—all the glory and praise belong to You! May these stories bless readers around the world and reap a mighty harvest for Your Kingdom during these troubled times.

To Loren Popineau, Senior Pastor of Family Worship Center Assembly of God Church in Littleton, Colorado, and his wife, Sylvia, for their consistent passion for prayer and lost souls. I hold their friendship dear.

To Larry York, Senior Pastor of Crossroads Baptist Church and his wife, Vicki, for sharing their passion for prayer and going beyond the walls of our church to reach the world for Christ—our current church home in The Woodlands, Texas.

To Stan Sullinger, Discipleship and Assimilation Pastor at Crossroads Baptist Church and his wife, Kima, whose wisdom and friendship have blessed me incredibly.

To Colin Milar, Founder of Igniting Prayer Action. His infectious passion for prayer refreshes the hearts of Christians on a global scale.

To Sharen Watson, Janetta Messmer, Linda Kozar, Janice Thompson, Heather Tipton, and Dannelle Woody for their steadfast friendship, encouragement, and expertise.

To Jim, my sweet husband and strongest supporter—bless you for your patience during some grueling hours, for grocery shopping, preparing countless meals, and being my sounding board. I love you.

To my daughter, Daniele—the most precious young woman in my life. Your strong, overcoming spirit of determination inspires and amazes me. You're a survivor. I love you.

To my family—Twilah, Lyla, Colleen, Annette, and Stuart—I am most blessed because of your love for me. I thank God for giving us godly parents and the gift of each other. To Mom and Dad Sharp, Kandy and Roger, you are loved and appreciated.

INTRODUCTION

⁓〰◉

MY FIRST EXPERIENCE with answered prayer occurred at the age of ten following a devastating loss in my young life. Alone and freezing on a darkened street, I whispered what was to me a prayer of gigantic proportions. It seemed unreasonable. Within minutes, God answered my whispered prayer. Awestruck and filled with excitement, I ran home to tell my family what had happened. In that moment I knew God was real and that He saw me, knew me, and loved me. This story is included in Chapter 6.

I grew up attending church three times a week, but allowed that habit to slip as a young adult. During a desperate time, overwhelmed with the consequences of my life choices, God made Himself known to me again in a real and personal way. The God of my childhood had not changed.

He picked up the pieces of my life, put them back together, and became the Anchor of my soul. He filled me with His Holy Spirit and sparked a passion to tell others that God still answers prayer.

One fall season in the course of my husband's job, we were transferred to Denver, Colorado. Once settled and the boxes unpacked, we found a small church nearby and, after a few visits, we knew it was where the Lord wanted us. We joined.

Those seven and a half years at Family Worship Center were deeply meaningful. Besides leading Bible studies, the Lord allowed me to be instrumental in birthing a weekly Saturday night prayer meeting. The attendance at those meetings revealed to us that God was at work in the life of our church. They continue to this day.

One night after the meeting, Sydney Redd, a faithful attendee, suggested we furnish a prayer list of needs for our meetings. Writing that prayer sheet helped me to become more sensitive to the needs of those in our body of believers.

As the weeks and months rolled by and as I continued compiling the weekly prayer list, I learned to ask the Lord to impress upon my heart needs and issues He wanted us to pray about. During one of those times of waiting before Him, a name came to mind that was far removed from my world. It was a moment of decision for me. Did I believe God had given me this name? After a search for the correct spelling, I added the name to the prayer sheet and that evening explained to our group that I believed God wanted us to pray for this person. We did.

The name remained on our list for many weeks.

Then one Tuesday morning the whole world knew the name—Osama bin Laden, the leader of the terrorist organization behind the 9/11 attacks on the World Trade Center, the Pentagon, and planes in flight.

Wednesday evening, frightened and anxious folks gathered in our church, packing the pews. Many were new faces to us. Pastor Popineau delivered a powerful yet comforting message. Among his words were these: "This tragic event did not happen behind God's back, for God sees and knows the thoughts and plans of every person's heart. In His goodness and mercy, our Saturday Night Prayer Group has been praying for this man."

In 2003, my husband's company moved us to Houston, Texas. We found a church home and joined. Still passionate about showing and telling the world that God answers prayer continues to beat strong in my heart. And compiling this book of answered prayer stories has been another moment of decision. Long ago I learned it is better to obey first and understand later.

I pray the book you hold in your hands blesses you and that your heart is moved to discover the plans God has for your life. His plans are tailor-made and unique to you, because He's the one who knows you best. "For You did form my inward parts; You did knit me together in my mother's womb" (Psalm 139:13 AMP).

Step outside your comfort zone and follow Him. *Hope, Pray, Believe,* and look back on a a life filled with meaning and purpose.

WORK IS GOOD FOR THE SOUL

In God's Time

WHEN THE ECONOMY takes a turn for the worst, many are affected by unemployment. Such was the case for my son. After more than a decade in the automotive industry, his work world turned upside down when he lost his job. He and his wife were expecting their second child, and he was forced to take whatever job he could find to keep them financially afloat. The only position he could find at the time was in the construction industry—building block walls.

Unaccustomed to manual labor, his back ached in protest to the new job, and his bank account protested in its own way too. The longer he went without his customary employment, the more his faith in God's provision began to fizzle. He had doubts about finding long-term employment again and lost confidence in his ability to succeed in anything else he might pursue. As the weeks went by, his prayers sounded more like "Hurry God!" instead of "Hurray God!"

"My skills are limited, Mom. Why would anyone want to hire a man like me?" His voice came across tired and flat. His eyes to the floor, he reminded me of the boy in school waiting to be chosen for the team—only to be the last one waiting.

Lord, give me words that will encourage. "Dan, do you remember going to Sunday school in Grandma Ginny's living room?"

"I remember," he said. I smiled as my grown son closed his eyes and folded his hands in his lap, just the way Grandma Ginny taught all the grandchildren to do. "Do unto others as you would have others do unto you," he recited. "See? Grandma Ginny would be proud of me." She made the kids recite the Golden Rule each week, until it was permanently ingrained in their little minds.

"Do you remember what else she taught you?"

"When life is most difficult and faith is hard to find, God will work everything out in His time." The words poured over his lips with the same lyrical quality Grandma Ginny used when she taught it. "I remember."

Over the next few months, I continued praying for my son and his family. Circumstances hadn't changed, but I noticed a glint of hope in Dan's attitude.

On one unusually warm autumn morning, I stopped at a garage sale, intent on making one woman's trash this woman's treasure. When I went to pay for my purchases, I was astonished. "Oh, my gosh! I haven't seen you in ages. How are you, Diane?" In between customers, my friend and I caught up. "Are you still working for the same company?"

"Unfortunately, no," she said. "They folded. Can you believe it? After twenty-five years, they just closed up shop."

"I'm sorry. The economy is hard on so many right now, isn't it?" I told her about my son's struggles to find employment after working for the same company for more than ten years.

"I was lucky to get into a good job fairly quickly after I was laid off. A utility company just happened to be hiring at the same time."

"Do you know if they're still hiring?"

"I don't know, but tell your son to stop by and put in an application. I can't do anything to get him hired, but if they ask, I'll put in a good word." We chatted a bit more as I made my purchase. Eager to let Dan know, I headed right home to make the call.

As the weeks wore on, Dan told me that he had almost given up hope of being called for an interview, not just with the utility company but with any company at all. He continued with hard labor—lifting heavy concrete blocks—wondering how much longer he could keep up the back-straining work. His muscles were overtaxed, and his medical insurance from the previous company was soon to expire. I've never seen my son under so much stress.

"What am I going to do, Mom? Carol is due in a few months, and without insurance we'll drown in debt."

The only thing I could do was encourage him. "In God's time . . . "

The following week, Dan received a call from the utility company. He interviewed and was hired for a ground-level position at half the wage he was used to receiving. But the job came with health benefits—and steady employment.

Dan later told me that his boss called him into the office during his first week and asked him about his family history. My son has a rather unique last name—twelve letters long—and he explained to me that his boss recognized it as one that sounded familiar to him. After running through a list of family members with the same name, the two of them finally made the connection. It turned out that his boss was married to one of my son's distant cousins. After they discovered they were family, Dan's superior told him that if he worked hard, he would be promoted, but only on his own merit and job performance, nothing more.

Just before winter, Dan had a great job evaluation. He was promoted to an indoor facility. He explained to me that his new position was somewhat hazardous, so at his wife's prompting he immediately applied for another job within the company. His boss understood my son's reservations, but told Dan that the position he put in for wouldn't open for a year. Fortunately though, he was first on the list. Poor consolation to my son, but at least in the meantime he had steady employment and hope for future advancement.

Dan visited his Grandma Ginny frequently, keeping her informed of his work and family life. He told me he shared with her how disappointed he was that he'd have to wait at least a year for the position he really desired.

"You know what Grandma Ginny told me today, Mom?"

I shifted the phone to my other ear, hugging it between my shoulder and chin. "What's that?"

"She said, 'You remember what your Grandma always told you—in God's time, not our own.'"

I smiled at the familiar words. "She's a smart woman. You'd best listen to her."

Two months later, Grandma Ginny became seriously ill and passed away. While attending her funeral, Dan reminded me of her counsel to him just a couple of months earlier. Although nothing had changed on the job, I could tell by the sound of his voice that his hope was fading. "In God's time . . ."

"Not our own." I followed.

At the conclusion of the memorial service, my son's cell phone rang. He walked a little distance away, but soon turned toward me. His expression was one of shock.

Not more bad news. He'd been through so much that I didn't think he'd be able to handle anymore.

"You're not going to believe this."

"What? What's happened?"

"That was a lady from the human resource department. I've been promoted. Not only that, they are going to pay for my schooling."

I hugged my son and repeated the words we had spoken only moments before. "In God's time, not our own."

My times are in your hands.

(Psalm 31:15a)

—*Linda O'Connell*

FINDING GOLD

Panic crawled over my shoulders and slithered down my arms at the rapid approach of the eighteen-wheeler's image in my rearview mirror. A heavy-duty cattle truck rocked back and forth just inches away in the lane to my right, and a Greyhound bus kept an even clip on my left. Options limited, I floored the accelerator and shot into the lane ahead of the cattle truck. The speedometer read way outside my comfort zone, evidenced by my white-knuckled grip on the steering wheel.

The escape route ahead—my exit—brought a welcome measure of relief. To say I was grateful seems inadequate. *Will I ever get used to driving like a maniac?* Bumper-to-bumper traffic on Houston's I-45 freeway lived up to its nightmare reputation. In Denver—our previous home—traffic wasn't even in the same league.

A few weeks later, early in September, I took our car in for its regular maintenance check at the local dealership. Their estimated time for service was upwards of two hours, so I used the time to browse their new SUVs during the wait. I cringed at the gas mileage and sticker prices on the eight-cylinder models. But the six-cylinder caught my attention.

I caught the reflection of a salesman headed my way. "Would you like to test drive one?" he asked.

I admitted an interest, but explained the actual reason behind my showroom visit.

"I'm sure you have better things to do than wait for your car. Why don't you let me arrange for you to take our demo and we'll call you when your car is ready?" I swallowed the bait.

Minutes later, a beautiful champagne-colored, six-cylinder SUV zipped into the empty parking space just outside the door. The driver exited the vehicle and tossed the keys to the salesman as we walked outside. He opened the door, gave me a few pointers, and I drove away.

Unbelievable. I ran my hand over the smooth leather seat, located my favorite classical radio station, and headed toward the highway. *Wow!* The sturdy feel, the elevation in proximity to the road. The view. I felt far less vulnerable. And as the dealership disappeared behind me, the truth hit me. We needed this car.

I also knew we weren't about to pay sticker price. *Lord, if it's okay with You, will You make a way for us to purchase a car like this?* I mulled over the costs and the burden of the payment. Then it dawned on me. My brother, Stuart, worked in the car business—in Tulsa. I decided I'd give him a call later in the evening.

I waited until after dinner to make the call. "Hey, Stuart."

"Jeanette. How are you?" My brother's cheerful tone made me smile.

"I'm well. You?

"Great. To what do I owe the privilege of this phone call?" I explained my desire—and need—for the SUV I'd driven earlier that day.

"So would you keep your eyes open for one? I'm looking for low mileage too."

"You and everyone else." My brother laughed. "Those vehicles are as scarce as hen's teeth. If you can find one down there, you better buy it." We talked on a bit, and then he asked, "Do you know what color you want? And do you want the Limited?"

"After careful thought, I do know what I want; it has to be a light color. I want leather seats, and, yes, we want the Limited."

When I hung up, I talked with my husband, Jim. We had discussed a change of vehicles in previous conversations and were in agreement. Now was the time. As we continued chatting, the thought crossed my mind that God knew the location of every one of those vehicles, and He could complete the arrangement, even if it was like looking for a needle in a haystack. I knew in the depths of my being the vehicle I wanted was out there and the Lord saw it even before I asked.

In the weeks that followed, I spoke with Stuart often and listened as he told me about the desperate economic state of the car business. Selling cars had been his life for the past twenty-plus years. "The industry's future never looked so dismal." Despair and concern laced his speech, and any words of encouragement I could offer seemed to ring hollow.

In that moment, the Lord dropped a prayer into my heart. *Father, would You find the right vehicle through my brother? How wonderful it would be to provide a sale and delivery through Stuart. After all, someone will sell it to us. Why not him?*

From that point, our SUV took on biblical proportions. I wanted God to bless Stuart with the sale. *This borders the magnitude of God parting the Red Sea, given the current economic crunch.* I forced the thought out of my head. I believed God's faithfulness to be the same now as it was then.

Jim and I had scheduled a trip to Tulsa to visit family in February, just a few short weeks away. I began to pray God would deliver our car while we were there. It made perfect sense—to me.

The day of our departure, and after we were on our way, I called Stuart. When he picked up, I said, "Just checking in. Has our SUV arrived yet?"

"No. Nothing new to report. I've phoned everyone I know. A few days ago, a man traded a black Limited in, but another salesman had a buyer and sold it that very day. Not one to be found. I've even checked my out-of-state contacts."

"Well, we're not there yet," I said. "Have faith and don't worry. It's on its way."

The drive from our home in North Houston to Tulsa typically took us about seven hours, but Jim and I decided to stop and visit our daughter, Daniele, who lives in Dallas. We met up with her at one of our favorite restaurants. Two hours later, we smothered her with love and resumed our drive.

Anxious to check the status of our new car, I speed-dialed Stuart again. "Has my car shown up yet?"

"I've been watching, but I haven't heard of or seen anything close to yours yet."

I laughed and said, "Lighten up. We're not there yet. It'll be there when we arrive."

He changed the subject. "How's the weather there?"

"Cold. I just put on my jacket and turned up the heater. I wish I had a wind gauge. The gusts out here are wicked."

"Well, drive safe and take your time," he said.

As the glare of the afternoon sun faded, I removed my sunglasses. We crossed the state line into Oklahoma, and I tilted my seat back to take a nap.

The ring of Jim's cell phone woke me. A glance at the clock on the dashboard read four o'clock. A slow grin spread across his lips as he listened. "Hold on, let me pass the phone to Jeanette."

"Hello." As I listened, a huge smile cascaded across my own face. "Consider it sold," I said. "We'll be in to sign the papers around seven this evening."

After I ended the call, I turned to my husband, "An auto-transport truck pulled up at the dealership. No one knew it was coming, not even the manager. Stuart saw it first and ran out to inspect the shipment. He pulled the tarp off, and there among the vehicles was a light-colored, Limited SUV. He couldn't believe it."

We stopped at Jim's folks for supper—homemade stew and hot cornbread. Then we headed over to the dealership to meet with Stuart and take a look at our new SUV. It was perfect. In fact, it was an exact replica of the one I test drove in Houston. It had a little over 11,000 miles on it and was in pristine condition.

"You can pick it up about ten tomorrow morning. By then it will be detailed and ready for the road," he said with a smile as big as Dallas. We completed the paperwork the next day and drove off the lot with our brand new SUV.

But God wasn't finished. He had bigger blessings in store for Stuart. Later that afternoon, a couple that attended Stuart's church came in looking for a smaller vehicle. Stuart showed them the car we had just traded in, and they bought it on the spot—a double blessing.

With God's help, we paid the loan off years before it was due.

May the words of my mouth and the meditation of my heart be pleasing in your sight, O Lord, my Rock and my Redeemer.

(Psalm 19:14)

—Jeanette Sharp

BEST FRIENDS

Lord, didn't You hear me? I wanted a miracle, not a job. The words tumbled out of my mouth as I hung up the phone. The employment agency had just informed me that I was now a full-time employee of Best Signs Systems. Along with the new job, I would continue to run the Rusty Moose Bed and Breakfast with my husband.

The logical side of my brain—*and* my husband—had been telling me I needed a job. The short tourist season that ran from Memorial Day to Labor Day didn't pay the bills. However, since I'm the stubborn sort, I continued to pray for the bed and breakfast to produce the income we needed. It didn't, and now I had a job I didn't want. *So much for a miracle.*

Monday morning, my first day of work, came much too quickly for my liking, and I was nervous about leaving the Rusty Moose. "What if a customer calls and I'm not here to answer the phone?"

My husband assured me everything would be fine and ushered me toward the door.

"What if Harry answers the phone?" Harry was the previous owner of the Rusty Moose, who had stayed on to help us after we purchased the place.

"I told him you'd check the messages on your lunch hour. Don't worry. He won't answer the phone. Everything will be fine." I nodded and headed off to work.

On the way, I prayed for another miracle, but I used a different angle this time. *Lord, I know I can reach more people at the bed and breakfast than at a sign company. What good am I going to be at Best Signs Systems?* Silence filled the cab of my tiny pick-up. *Okay, Lord. You're in control.* I pulled into the parking lot and reluctantly walked through the door of my new employer's office.

"Good morning, Janetta!" Bonnie greeted me with a warm smile and showed me to my desk. She patiently explained my responsibilities. I had no idea how much detail went into making a simple bathroom sign. By the third day of my new job, I was settling in quite nicely. And Ray was right. Stopping in to check messages during my lunch hour worked out just fine.

That is, it worked just fine until I heard Harry's conversation on the recorder with a potential customer.

"Rusty Moose Bed and Breakfast."

A chipper customer on the other end of the line responded, "Yes, I'd like to make a reservation, please." To which Harry responded, "Owners are at work. You'll have to call back later. Oh, and by the way, I built this B&B! It's a great house. Call back about 5:00. They'll be back then." I was confused by the conversation, so I can't imagine what the customer was thinking. "Uh, okay. Thanks." And the message ended.

Lord, please help me control the urge to inflict bodily harm on Harry right now! I ate a quick lunch and went back to the sign company.

Bonnie, my supervisor, asked me if something was wrong. I guess my heavy sighs, compounded by intense pounding on the keyboard, gave me away. I told her about the phone message. At the end of my story, I added, "Do you know how much time a person gets for justifiable homicide? And will you come visit me in jail?" She laughed, but all I wanted to do was cry.

Just then, my new boss, Sally, rushed around the corner. "Who's going to jail?" *Why must I always blurt out every word that comes to mind?* I recapped the story for Sally and reiterated the "justifiable homicide" part. I made a big joke about it, because I didn't want her to think I was bringing my other business problems to her business.

"Janetta, if you need to forward your phone calls here, you can. Whatever you need to do, we'll help you." Sally put her arm around me and patted my shoulder. I sat in stunned silence and then whispered, "Thank you." I wiped away threatening tears.

"Whatever you need to do, Janetta. We want your B&B to succeed." Sally wrapped me in a warm hug. *Unbelievable, Lord. Looks like things are going to work out after all.*

Unfortunately, not all things worked out regarding the bed and breakfast. Six months after I started my job at Best Signs Systems, Ray and I found out the property we'd purchased lacked the proper building permits. For the next year, we battled with both the county and the previous owner; but because of the mounting costs of having the permits finalized, the Rusty Moose Bed and Breakfast closed its doors.

Through it all, I continued my job at the sign company. Each morning I thanked the Lord for giving me this special place during one of the most turbulent times of my life. Most days, I'd go to work and keep generally quiet about the events surrounding the B&B. My job—for a few hours—was a place I could forget our property problems. But some days, when things became overwhelming and I needed someone to talk to, my "best" friends were there.

As the saying goes, "All good things must come to an end."

After September 11, 2001, Ray applied for a job with the Transportation Security Administration. He accepted a position with them in Houston, Texas, which meant a move—and leaving Best Sign Systems. I'd grown so attached, I couldn't imagine life without them. My last day came, and all I could do was hug everyone—with tears. "You guys have no idea how much I appreciate you. I'm going to miss you so much."

"We're going to miss you too." Sally wiped a rogue tear. "You've been such a blessing to all of us. You're a true example of how to go through difficult times with grace."

"Oh, Sally, it wasn't me. I couldn't have done it without the Lord's help or all of you." As I left Best Sign Systems, I realized the Lord gave me my miracle. Maybe not the one I prayed for, but the one He gave me. It was so much better than I could have ever asked for. *Thank You, Lord, for my "best" friends.*

> "Because he loves me," says the LORD, "I will rescue him; I will protect him, for he acknowledges my name. He will call upon me, and I will answer him; I will be with him in trouble, I will deliver him and honor him.
>
> (Psalm 91:14-15)

—*Janetta Messmer*

A MATCH MADE IN HEAVEN

Layoff. The word buzzed up and down the halls of the bank where I worked. Years before, the bank had lost money on failed loans. Now, in the late eighties, their steady decline aligned them for purchase by an out-of-state holding company.

My coworkers groaned. A layoff signaled the end to the work they loved. Morale sank, but the employees showed up every day and concentrated on their tasks. I saw the impending layoff as a release from a prison and a new beginning.

For two years I endured physical and emotional stress from my job in purchasing. I couldn't wait to leave it—even if it meant starting all over somewhere else. Still, I wondered, *Where will I go? What will I do?*

I started at the bank right after college. During more than twelve years there, I earned a healthy salary and enjoyed good benefits. But when the pressure in purchasing grew too intense, I dreamed of sacking groceries for minimum wage. Anything to escape the stress.

With a layoff on the horizon, I took a personal inventory: a degree in English and a love of words. Maybe these could lead me to something in publishing, like editing. But could I, a single lady, support myself doing something I loved?

Deciding to trust God with the gifts He gave me, I prayed for a job in editing. Once my severance pay ran out in April 1989, I filed for unemployment and made contacts every week to find work. As summer approached, nothing had opened up.

Knowing of my word skills, a friend suggested I consult a book at the library that listed publishing jobs in my state. As I sat at the table and flipped pages, a librarian walked by.

"What are you looking for?" he asked. When I told him, he walked over to a nearby shelf. "You don't want that book," he told me and handed me another volume: *Grade's Book of Publications.* I turned to my city and state and found the title of a Christian magazine. No street address—just a post office box number.

I dashed home and zipped off the same letter of introduction and résumé I'd sent to a dozen other companies. I told myself it was a complete waste of time, but desperation pushed me. My unemployment money would run out in a few weeks.

I mailed the letter and résumé and prepared for another rejection. I thought of calling an agency for temporary work. At least I could bring in a little money while I waited for full-time work.

During prayer time one morning I asked God about my idea. *Will I mess up Your plans if I call the temp agency?*

Deep in my spirit, a nearly audible voice shouted, *Yes!*

His answer made no sense to me. What's wrong with bringing in a little money? Still, I obeyed. A few days later, I thought my obedience had paid off. A Christian publishing company two hours from my home announced an opening for a copy editor. The drive would be a long one if I got the job, but at least I could use my skills and education.

However, they didn't prepare me for part of the interview. I had to take a copyediting test to be considered for the job. Those strange correction marks on paper looked like a foreign language to me. I did my best on the test, but inside I knew I blew it.

As I drove home after the interview, desperation mounted within me. Seven months of job searching had drained my energy and confidence. I ignored the emphatic voice I'd heard in prayer days before. *You're out of time,* I told God. *If the phone doesn't ring this afternoon about a job, I'm calling the temp agency tomorrow.*

But when I got home, a message on my answering machine was waiting. The man himself—the editor at the Christian magazine I'd contacted two weeks before. When I returned his call, he asked, "How did you know we were looking for someone? We haven't told anyone outside our organization that we need to hire."

How did I know? I didn't, but God did.

As it turned out, the magazine had been looking to fill an editorial position for a year but hadn't found anyone with the right qualifications—until I came along. Within a week after my interview with the editor, the waiting ended, and I got the job that God prepared for me.

That was twenty years ago. I'm now associate editor of that magazine, working with words and experiencing each day the hope and future God had for me all along.

"For I know the plans I have for you," declares the LORD, "plans to prosper you and not to harm you, plans to give you hope and a future."

(Jeremiah 29:11)

—*Sherri Langton*

SHOW ME, LORD

I have always been told that according to the Bible we are not to ask for signs when we desire something. I'm not from Missouri, but sometimes I have to say, *Show me, Lord. Help me in my unbelief.*

At the dinner table one evening my husband said, "I'm considering applying for the Chief of Police position in another city. What do you think?"

I said, "You are my husband, and wherever you go, I will also go."

He got the word out to his network of associates in the law enforcement community. Soon, letters and calls started coming in with requests for his résumé. We didn't know the process could take as long as a year from receiving the call or letter requesting his résumé to filling the position.

My husband submitted his résumé, and finally we began to receive letters from different cities notifying us that he was a finalist. When that happened, he would be asked to come to that city to be interviewed by the mayor or city manager, police officials, police unions, and community leaders. Some interviews lasted two days.

Each time, we trekked to the library to research that particular city.

Most cities encouraged him to bring me along so we could assess whether or not we wanted to live there. Unfortunately, when the process was over months later, he came in second or third. This went on for about five years.

Since it was public record, his selection as a finalist would be printed in the newspaper. Sometimes it made the local television news. His embarrassment grew when he met people who said, "I thought you were in *so and so* city."

One evening he said, "I'm not going to apply anymore. This is just too hard to handle. And those in the department who are in line for my job are giving me the evil eye. They want my job."

A few days later I went to the mailbox and found a letter from the City of Chattanooga, Tennessee. When my husband came home from work, I said, "There's another letter."

"Forget it; I'm never doing that again."

"We've prayed about this, and if we believe that God's in control, then you need to submit your résumé."

He fumed a few days before he said, "Okay, you can send it, but I'm not doing any research. I'm going in with no preparation, and if God wants me to have the job, He'll have to do the work."

I sent off the paperwork, and we received a letter notifying him that he was a finalist. I was unable to go with him, so he went alone.

It was a two-day interview, and the cream-of-the-crop candidates were asked to stay a second day. Of the original ninety-eight who applied, there were eight to ten finalists, but only two or three got the second-day opportunity. I didn't hear from him until he returned home.

When he walked in the door, he didn't look like a happy camper. I thought—*I'll never live this one down.* Finally, I worked up the nerve to ask, "How did it go?"

"The mayor offered me the job."

I jumped up, shouting, "Hallelujah!"

"Hold on," he said. "I told him no."

"You did *what*? After all these years, you get an offer and you turned it down?"

"Yes, and I told the mayor I would come only if I could bring God with me. He said that was fine with him. Then I said, 'Do your background checks and complete your interviews with the other candidates. If you still want me, call me.'

"The mayor said he didn't know anything about policing, but he'd have my back. All I needed to do was tell him what I needed, and he'd work to get it for me."

Again, we waited for the process to unfold, telling no one. It was a very trying time for me—so much at stake. If we moved, I would have to leave my mother, who lived in a nursing home, and my twin sister, who was divorced and had many health issues.

I would leave behind my job of thirty years, my community, and the church I loved—even the sports teams I loyally followed. I'd made many friends in those thirty years.

Lord, are You a part of this, or is this my husband looking for a career move and asking You to bless it? Show me that You are really a part of it.

I needed a sign. The only thing I could think to ask for was to see the word Chattanooga in large print somewhere in Houston, Texas. I looked everywhere I thought I might see it—license plates, bumper stickers, everywhere—but to no avail.

One day I was on a commuter bus riding home from work when the traffic stalled. As I waited, I looked through the window and spotted a truck going in the opposite direction. The truck was white with red and blue trim. It looked as if it were shining because it was so white. I saw the name of the company—Covenant Transport.

Why would a trucking company have a name with a biblical connotation?

I knew *covenant* meant God's promise to His people and *transport* meant to take something from one place to another. I glanced at the door of the cab to see where the truck was from. It was from Chattanooga, Tennessee.

"Praise God, we're going to Chattanooga!"

I began praying for the department to receive my husband and his Christian beliefs, for us to have Christian neighbors, a good church family, and good Christian friends. God answered every one of my prayers.

The Lord's blessings continued at my husband's new job. One officer initiated a Bible study, the chaplaincy program grew, and closet Christians came to the forefront. Staff meetings began with prayer.

During that time, I served on a board that used privately funded money to pay for teachers to teach the Bible in junior and senior high schools. I had the privilege of speaking to groups and giving my testimony. This included churches of all denominations, all ethnic groups, and all economic levels. I also led people to Christ, something I'd never done before.

One of the highlights of my husband's career in Chattanooga came at a luncheon fellow officers gave to honor an officer who had terminal pancreatic cancer. The man gave his testimony, and more than thirty police officers gave their lives to Christ.

I did get a chance to meet the president of Covenant Transport—a Christian-based company. Each of the company trucks displays an anti-abortion slogan on its rear door.

When I needed assurance, Jesus gave me blessed assurance. I have no doubt whatsoever that God sent us to Chattanooga, Tennessee. I grew more spiritually in the seven years we were there than I did my whole life, and my husband received Jesus as his Lord and Savior—a step beyond walking down the aisle when he was nine years old.

I don't need signs for everything God asks me to do. But I do know that He leads me and sustains me wherever I am. I give Him all of the honor, the glory, and the praise forever!

God blessed and used my husband and me in Chattanooga. We will always hold that city in our hearts and be grateful for what He did through us there. To God be the glory for all the things He has done!

He remembers his covenant forever, the word he commanded, for a thousand generations.

(I Chronicles 16:15)

—*Elsa Dotson*

SUCCESS—JUST A PRAYER AWAY

I couldn't think too hard about what I was about to do—a book signing. However, I knew if I hurried to my quaint little neighborhood bookstore, opened the door confidently, and greeted a few people, I'd probably be okay. So that's what I did, and it went pretty well. Then I looked at the large pile of books on the small table set aside for the author and picked one up. I knew I had to think about what should be written on the flyleaf. Just about everyone who bought a book would want a few special words or the ever popular "To my good friend so and so" followed by the author's signature penned with a flourish.

A sigh escaped my lips, but I was doing all right. Okay, I was a little shaky. Next came the moment to actually speak, and my old problem reared its ugly head. I could feel the heat snake up from my stomach, surge into my chest, explode onto my neck, and by the time the book was signed my cheeks were in full blaze—autumn red. It was a struggle, but I straightened my shoulders and spoke.

"This is the first children's book I've ever had signed by the author," I blurted.

That's right. I was having a picture book signed for my two grand-daughters. You thought I was signing my own book, didn't you? I wish. The thing is, if I'd gone there only to have the book signed, I would have been fine. But I was a quaking wreck because I'd also gone for another reason. I wanted to see how that author was handling the situation.

I wanted to mention my own soon-to-be-published picture book and thought we might even have a moment or two of jovial author-to-author chitchat. But nope, there was no time for that. I had presumed too much. She was a busy bee, laughing with the children, talking with the parents, and signing book after book. I stepped quietly away, and even though I managed to get out of the store without actually passing out, I was quite disappointed—in myself.

You see, I'm one of those people whose nervousness shows up as an embarrassing physical manifestation. My neck and face turn deep scarlet, and as soon as someone says, "Do you know your face is beet red?" I lose all concentration. This has been my agonizing hurdle since about eighth grade, the year my mother convinced me to take a speech and drama class to gain self-confidence.

For the brief time I was at that book signing, the author was as sweet as she could be. But the very idea of talking to her about my book had me quivering like Gumby in a microwave. As I watched her interaction with the eager book buyers, my first thought was, *I could never do that. I'd be blotchy red the whole time, my hands would shake, and in a million years I could never do that.*

Several days later, in the process of an in-the-mirror-self-analysis we all do, I remembered reading a theory that stated shy people are often extremely self-centered. That seemed like a harsh assessment, but I thought it might apply to me. Perhaps I had a shyness problem, and I irrationally imagined big eyes on me all the time, scrutinizing my every move, so I'd better be careful and not mess up.

Why, I might be in a restaurant, drop a fork, and have the waiter's booming voice announce the presence of a super klutz to every taco-eater in the room! How could I ever bear up under the glares? Well, that probably won't happen. Even though I don't think of myself as shy exactly, I wondered if I was so self-centered that my own body reacted with a flushed neck and face. This was a problem no writer needed to be saddled with. After all, I needed to be able to promote myself and sell my work, especially the writing I did for children.

So I set my mind to the task, and one of my strategies actually worked. I prayed. You might be thinking, *Oh, for crying out loud! What kind of help is that?* For me, it was help that worked. The supreme test came at the performance of my play, "Bartholomew the Clueless Shepherd," that I'd been coaxed into writing for our Sunday school. I knew the church would be packed. I knew my name would be announced as the author of the play, and I knew people would look around to see if I was there.

I also knew that bargaining with God is a no-no, but I couldn't help myself. I prayed, *Lord, if You want me to be a writer, then I need to be rid of this flushing problem.* I prayed fervently not to be self-centered and nervous. I asked to see only the children, teachers, and parents and to be a happy, grateful participant in the whole event. I truly wanted *me* out of the way.

Well, you know, I think God must pass out temporary steel spines to people like me, because when the Sunday of the performance rolled around, my inner calm amazed me. I remained relaxed through the whole thing and afterwards took the kudos and congratulations with grace—or at least that's how it felt. Sure, I got a little red, but only a little.

My prayer was answered beautifully, and it was glorious, like a lead cape dropping from my shoulders, and I have to believe that the inner steel and grace stayed long enough for me to submit the play to a publisher. The positive feedback from the kids, teachers, and parents made me bold. The only joy that surpassed the joy of overcoming my embarrassing hurdle was the joy I felt when CSS Publishing bought that play the following spring and published it a few years later. Now, if I can only conquer bookstore visits, I think I may be able to call myself a writer. You'd better believe I'll be praying about it.

He answered their prayers, because they trusted in him.
(I Chronicles 5:20b)

—*Susan Sundwall*

PRAYER CONFIRMATION

Sometimes, God's leading doesn't make sense, and Sunday morning was no exception. *Lord, You know I can't fit another thing into my schedule. I don't have enough time to write more or market my book.* I lingered in the lady's room, pouring my heart out to God before Sunday school started. I didn't see how I could add one more thing to my calendar.

You can give up teaching the ladies Bible study.

What? Not teach the Bible study? *Where did that come from? What about the many women who attended the study? And attendance is on the increase. Am I hearing you right, Lord? Why would You want me to leave teaching? I can't imagine not leading the study.*

When I finished my mini-tantrum, I reconsidered. *But if this is Your plan, then I need some confirmation.* I left the powder room and made my way to class with more questions than answers.

After our lesson, my husband and I assumed our post as church greeters. We hug necks and shake hands with equal gusto; it's second nature to us.

We're acquainted with just about everyone at our church, so when someone new arrives, we're quick to recognize a visitor. "Welcome! We're glad to have you with us today." My husband spied the new couple and joined me in giving them a hardy greeting.

"Thank you," the lady said. "We're in town visiting our children."

"Where are you from?" I recognized the woman's Texas accent—but it wasn't a south Texas accent.

"We live in Tyler."

"Really? We have grown kids that live on Lake Tyler. Do you live near there?"

"Nearby. Whenever you venture north to visit your kids, give us a call. We'd love to introduce you to our neck of the woods." Carol handed me her business card.

During the service, I felt the urge to speak with her again before she left. After the service, I found her in the foyer. "I feel our connection may be for a future purpose. Here's my card, just in case."

"I get the same impression."

After I introduced her and her husband to others in our church, she motioned me to a quiet corner. "Charlotte, I know we just met, but I believe the Lord has something He'd like to share with you. I believe He wants you to know it's okay to lay down some of the things you're doing and let go. Others can handle your responsibilities. He wants you to step through open doors and do things you've never done before. I believe He's talking about a whole different ministry."

This woman didn't know me or anything about my restroom chat with the Lord earlier in the morning or the fact that I led Bible studies. She knew I had children in Tyler Lake; and I'd mentioned briefly that I was a writer. That was all—vague information at best. But her visit with me that day answered questions that had plagued me only two hours earlier.

Later that week, I approached Alice. "Would you like to lead the ladies Bible study?"

Puzzled by my request, Alice responded, "Why? Don't you want to teach anymore?"

"I believe the Lord wants me to devote more time to writing and marketing the book I've written." As the words spilled from my mouth, I knew without a doubt it was God's will.

"I knew God would move you into a full-time writing ministry," Alvie, another longtime member of my Bible study, said.

Others made similar comments. Any one or all of them could have told me what the woman from Tyler said. But would I have listened to someone I knew? God chose to speak to me through a stranger.

On the way home, I stopped at Macy's make-up counter. Toni, one of the clerks, came to my assistance. "Mrs. Holt, how are you?"

"Blessed. How about you?"

"Me too." As we continued our conversation, I shared my news with her. Several minutes later, my purchases secured, I turned to leave.

"Wait a moment, I want to give you something." Toni said as she walked to another counter and disappeared behind a cubicle. I expected her to return with a fistful of product samples, but instead, she handed me a jeweled cross. "I want you to have this."

Breathtaking! "No one's ever given me a more beautiful cross." My voice faltered over the lump in my throat. "I'll think of you whenever I wear this." I hugged her.

"One more errand to run," I announced to no one in particular as I strolled toward my car. My husband needed some shirts dry-cleaned.

The Christian bookstore was in the same shopping center, and since they were hosting an upcoming book signing for me, I decided to stop in and check on last-minute details. Before I left my car, I gently tucked the cross into a lined pocket of my purse.

The bell jingled when I entered the store, and I smiled at the sweet sound. While waiting for a clerk to help me, I recognized another customer but couldn't quite place where I had met her. "Don't I know you?"

"I'm Jane Davis."

"Oh, I remember. You're the one who makes the lovely angel pins."

She reached into her bag and pulled out her latest creation—a small cross. "The owner of the store is test-marketing this piece for me."

"It's absolutely beautiful." After a brief conversation, I finished my business with the clerk and left.

While starting my car and dropping the gear into reverse, I spied Jane in my rearview mirror frantically waving at me.

"Here, I want you to have this." She handed me one of her magnificent crosses, smiled, got into her vehicle, and drove away. I was stunned. She was the second person in one day to gift me a cross.

Lord, two people I barely know gave me crosses today. Are You trying to show me something? A wave of pleasure swept over me. He was showing me His pleasure with my obedience in giving up something I loved—teaching Bible study—to venture into an unknown territory of a full-time writing ministry.

Follow me. Take up your cross and follow me. Words whispered from the Lord to my heart.

The words of the visitor from Tyler, my obedience in giving up teaching, the two women bearing crosses as gifts. Each one held significance in my journey.

> Trust in the Lord with all you heart and lean not on your understanding; in all your ways acknowledge him, and he will make your paths straight.
>
> (Proverbs 3:5-6)

—Charlotte Holt

Prayer Nugget

Prayer opportunities are present around us. We just don't recognize them. When we hear someone comment about a troublesome issue in his or her life, take the initiative and ask, "Could I pray with you?" Prayer brings God's power into the center of their need.

Ask the Lord to make you sensitive to hurting people around you. A simple prayer will do. *Father, I ask You to give me a holy boldness to step outside my comfort zone and become Your hands, Your feet, Your heart to a hurting world. In Jesus' name, I pray. Amen.*

_____

_____

_____

_____

_____

_____

_____

_____

_____

_____

_____

_____

_____

_____

_____

_____

_____

_____

Chapter 2

NO WORRIES

THE COLLISION

WE ASKED FOR protection, but not necessarily for wisdom. With our heads bowed and hands folded, our peaceful prayer circle could not have contrasted more with the weather. Outside, the snow fell thick and heavy, like the inside of a snow globe. And the wind blew so hard it seemed as if the snow came from the east rather than the sky.

"Anybody think we shouldn't go?" asked our professor.

It was an honest question. He wanted our thoughts. Our agenda for the day included a field trip that could not be rescheduled. With that fact in mind, we all remained silent and stared at our feet. No one wanted to be that fearful voice of safety that would keep everyone from enjoying the day ahead.

Having ignored our one opportunity to turn back, we filed outside, one after another. A frigid wind rushed past us. I hugged my coat closer as our small class squeezed into a van and two cars.

I took a seat in the back of the first car. We drove without much conversation. Music flooded the air, and small-talk filled in the gaps. With headphones in my ears, I was left to my own thoughts. And one kept sneaking into my mind—how uncomfortable my seatbelt felt. It stretched over my waist like a belt two sizes too small. I unbuckled it for a bit, but that made me the only person in the car without one. I buckled up again, keeping my complaints to myself.

The snow continued to fall without rest. If anything, it picked up. Visibility was reduced to whatever you could make out between the white flakes. Our driver pressed on, accelerator down.

Suddenly, a terrifying sight appeared in my line of vision. The van, which had been traveling at nearly fifty miles per hour right ahead of us, abruptly stopped. It seemed as if it had collided with an impenetrable wall. The van bucked and spun; its headlights soon faced directly at us. No one screamed. We didn't have time. I only sucked in a breath. And waited.

The collision came. The thunderous sound of metal on metal erupted. I was thrown forward with a force I'd never experienced before or since. The only thing keeping me inside the car was the seatbelt stretched across my waist. Direction became relative. We spun like a carnival ride, finally coming to a stop in a nearby ditch.

"Is everyone all right?" our driver asked.

That was a question I'd already asked myself. The initial answer was a simple no. My stomach throbbed, and each breath took effort. But before panic set in, the pain and my breathing eased. As far as I could tell, I was fine.

We sat still for only a few seconds. The faces of my fellow classmates quickly surrounded us. We stepped out into the cold. The snow swallowed our ankles and made its way up our shins as we stumbled forward.

The van was turned backward in the center of the road, and the car following us was nowhere to be found. As we stepped closer, the full range of damage came into view. The van's entire front end looked like a mangled, jagged mess. Our professor, who rode in the passenger seat, stepped out first. His eyes remained wide open, and a thick glob of blood clung to his mustache.

Molly, a student known best for her sarcasm, shed that persona. She took on the role of leader, barking orders through the confusion. She yelled for everyone to get out of the van. Her voice grew louder and louder as black smoke began drifting from the engine. A minute or two after the last student exited, I saw the flame, small and steady, like a campfire.

My instincts kicked in. I rushed to a semi parked just ahead of the wreck. I came back with the fire extinguisher, determined to do something heroic. But my feet stopped well short of the van. No need to run anymore. The small fire was now an out-of-control inferno, engulfing the hood and reaching ten feet in the air. I handed the fire extinguisher back, unused.

The next few hours passed in a quick blur. Everyone congregated in a nearby gas station. With hearts still racing, we talked about what just happened. Gradually, we pieced all the details together. The semi I borrowed the fire extinguisher from was what the van had hit. At the moment of impact, our professor sat sideways, his knees pointed toward the driver. Had he been facing forward, it's likely his legs would have been pinned by the wreckage, leaving him to the mercy of the flames.

The third car, which we'd almost forgotten about, said they swerved to avoid us but sideswiped another car. With all the horrific details, everyone walked—or at least limped—away from the accident. The worst injures involved full body bruises and sore backs.

We didn't ask for wisdom, but God gave it anyway. My seatbelt, the position of our professor's legs, and the speedy exit from the van all had God's fingerprint on them. They were answered prayers we hadn't bothered to send to the Lord. As I reflect on what happened, I can't help but think that God may not always give us what we want, but He always knows what we need.

> Let them give thanks to the Lord for his unfailing love and his wonderful deeds for men.
>
> (Psalm 107:15)

—Andrew Culbertson

Surrounded by Darkness

We were hurtling along a freeway. My mom was driving and my oldest sister was in the front seat. They chatted as I sat in the back quietly doing my schoolwork and keeping one ear open for anything interesting that might come up in their conversation. Tagging along while my mother dropped my sister off at university wasn't my favorite place to be on a Wednesday night, but it certainly beat staying home alone while the rest of my family carted off to their various midweek meetings and responsibilities.

I eventually grew bored with my schoolwork and the conversation, so I looked through the car window and watched the car lights whiz past us. Being recently born again, my mind was pondering different aspects of God and how He looked after His children. After this night, though, I would question no more His timely providence.

I gave a slight shiver as I thought of the darkness sweeping the city that we were approaching. Johannesburg, South Africa, was becoming more dangerous with every passing day. The violence and theft rates were horrific, especially at night. I hummed a tune and tried to push thoughts and stories about the danger of the city out of my mind. The stories were too terrifying for me to even think about.

After we dropped my sister off at college, my mom and I pulled to a stop in front of a well-lit store to wait until her class was over. My mom got out her book and I got out my schoolwork, determined to finish it, and determined to stamp out the fear that was enveloping my mind as the darkness outside encroached the city.

About an hour later, we got a text message that my sister was ready to be picked up. My mom started the car, and I breathed a sigh of relief. Finally, we could get out of this scary place.

My relief was short-lived, though, as the car sputtered and shook and could not be persuaded to start again. Fear seeped into my soul and threatened to overtake my whole body while all around us shops were being locked down and lights being switched off for the night. My mother called around to our church friends and different companies to see if anybody could tow us or help us. They were all apologetic, but for various reasons none of them could come.

As my mom ended the last phone call, an idea that I should have had earlier popped up. "Mom, why don't we pray?"

My mother agreed right away and started praying out loud for our car to start. I sent a quick, silent prayer up too, hoping with all my might that God was listening. I needn't have worried, though, for as my mom said the last "Amen" and tried to turn on the car for what seemed like the tenth time, it started.

While we drove out of the parking lot, I thanked God for answering our prayers, grateful that He cares enough to oversee each detail in our lives, even the seemingly insignificant ones. Though that story may not have seemed to be a big thing, it has stuck with me over the years, and I have acquired much encouragement from the fact that God cares about His children and still answers prayer today.

> But my God shall supply all your need according to his riches in glory by Christ Jesus.
>
> (Philippians 4:19 KJV)

—Danielle VanMeter

A Sudden Slip

Prayer has the power to change things; it has the power to heal. Studies show that many doctors believe in the power of prayer as well. Since I was a child, I too have believed in the power of prayer.

When I moved to this beautiful, hilly, rural area twenty-six years ago at the age of forty-six, I realized a lifelong dream. My children were grown and living lives on their own. It was finally my turn to live the life I had dreamed of, surrounded by God's beautiful creation.

And for over twenty-five years, I have done just that—roaming these hills and woods at will with my three dogs, enjoying the wildlife, and teaching my grandchildren about them when they come to visit from the city. It is a life I love and hope to continue for some time, even though my grown children think that as I age I should be moving closer to civilization.

Whenever the subject comes up, I tell them, "I'm not ready to give up my life in the country." So they got me a cell phone that I promised to have on me at all times when I'm not inside the house. Most of the time I've kept my promise, but you know how it is sometimes. We forget.

On December 10, 2005, my life changed in an instant. We had a light snowfall the day before, only a couple of inches, but enough to make things slippery outside. It was Saturday, and earlier that day, my friend Jan and I had an enjoyable time eating lunch at a Mexican restaurant and then shopping in a large department store.

I got home later than usual and rushed to feed the animals. I fed the three dogs and four cats and ushered them into the house for the night. I was almost ready to settle down too.

It was very late afternoon, and I noticed the bird feeders needed refilling. Cardinals, chickadees, gold and purple finches, and many other birds were waiting for their supper before settling down for another frigid night. So I went back out and walked up a small hill to get to the feeders, carrying a bag of wild birdseed.

Suddenly, I slipped and landed on my right side with a thud! I fully expected to get right back up and continue my walk to the feeders. But when I tried to get up, the worst pain I have ever experienced shot through my right side, making me cry out in pain. I quickly realized that I was not going to get to the feeders, or anywhere else for that matter!

It was already past four in the afternoon, and it would be dark in another hour. I had no neighbors close by who might see me and come to my aid. And I didn't have my cell phone with me! Panic gripped me as I realized that if I had to spend the night outside, I might freeze to death. I somehow had to find a way to get into the house.

Still trying to rely on my own strength, I repeatedly attempted to get up, with the same result: unbearable pain and no success.

Dear God, I'm in big trouble here, and I need Your help. Only You can help me now. I pray for Your wisdom and strength. Please help me get back into the house. I trust that You will help and sustain me, Lord.

Tears welled in my eyes as I prayed. Then, closing them, I lay there a while, feeling the chill of the snow that covered the earth beneath me, and slowly resigned myself to the inevitable—spending the night outside.

Suddenly, a soft whisper of a suggestion entered my head. *Try to crawl into the house. You will have the strength to do it. I will give you the strength.*

Oh, I don't know if I can, Lord. I don't know if I can, I whispered, tears streaming down my face.

You can if you try. Trust in Me and try, the voice urged.

When I was a little girl in Hungary during World War II, prayer had sustained me through many close calls. I believed I heard God's voice telling me how to stay safe during bombings and other scary occurrences. And now, I knew God was speaking to me again.

I decided to try to crawl up the hill toward my front door. Somehow, I managed to turn on my stomach, and using my arms and upper body, I also managed to move slowly toward my destination. There was excruciating pain with every move, but I kept pulling my lower body along.

It took me an hour to get to my front door, but as darkness descended I was finally able to make it into the warm house where I had turned on the lights before I went outside. Exhausted, I lay on the floor for a few minutes and rested. My dogs came to my side and licked my face.

"Go lie down, guys, while I try to get help," I pleaded with them. They did as I asked. They knew something was wrong.

When I was able to move again, I reached the sturdy wooden chair in the dining room and managed to pull myself up by holding onto its back. My cell phone was on the table. With shaking hands, I punched in my son's number.

"I'm hurt," I said to Greg. "I think I broke my hip. I need help," I cried into the phone in an anguished voice. "I'm in so much pain, I can barely stand it."

Fifteen minutes later a sheriff's deputy arrived, soon followed by an ambulance with its siren blaring. I live ten miles from town, and Greg, who lives 200 miles away, was on his way as well.

"The door is unlocked," I called out when I heard a knock. I was still standing in the dining room, holding on to the wooden chair with all my might. Within minutes I was in the ambulance, speeding toward the hospital. The kind female attendant quickly gave me a pain pill.

She asked, "How and where did you fall."

"I was outside, trying to fill the birdfeeders, and I slipped in the snow," I said.

"Outside? But how did you manage to get back into the house?"

"When I realized I couldn't make it in on my own, I asked God for help. He gave me the strength to make it into the house," I said, with grateful tears coursing down my cheeks. "Sometimes, it takes a crisis to make one realize once again that God is always near, and all we have to do is ask for His help. He will never let us down."

She nodded and stroked my head gently. After I was wheeled into the hospital, my vital signs checked, and X-rays taken, I was rolled into surgery, just before midnight. When I woke up in the recovery room, Greg was at my side.

"I called Joe and Andrea," he said, referring to my other children who live in Ohio. "Thank God you made it into the house, Mom. But you know you're supposed to have your cell phone with you whenever you're outside."

Dr. Joseph, the orthopedic surgeon, came to see me early the next morning. After hearing how I made it into the house on my own, he said, "You're a strong woman. I just put two pins in your hip!"

"My strength comes from God," I told him quietly; for I knew it did.

I was released from the hospital the third day, and my three grown children took turns taking care of me for six weeks, along with help from a visiting nurse and a therapist.

Now, four years later, I am fully recovered from my broken hip and able to walk and drive. I still live on my own in the country. All because He heard my prayers and came to my aid.

In my distress I called to the Lord; I cried to my God for help. From his temple he heard my voice; my cry came before him into his ears.

(Psalm 18:6)

—Renie Burghardt

MY DROWNING MOMENT

The mini-bus and its five weekend passengers wound its way through city streets until we could see emerald fields instead of smudged windowpanes. It slowed down to a pant as it dug its tire treads into a rising stone bridge. From the peak of the little hill I could see both sides of the river we would be canoeing down. To my left, an old mill stood guard over rapids that quickly returned to their sleepier state; to my right, a blue, 500-thread Egyptian sheet of water fitted tightly to her riverbanks.

"I'm going to drive farther up to a spot where we can put the canoes into the water," our headmistress and driver, Miss Mew, said. She looked relaxed and happy—an unusual sight when compared to our boarding-school weekdays.

The taller girls unpacked the canoes, and soon the pointed boats were rippling gently at the edge of the bank beside us, distressing the glass mirror of water. I puffed up my early-pubescent shape with a life jacket, stepped into the central hole of my spraydeck (a cover that prevents water entering the canoe), and cautiously planted two feet and then my rear into the body of my canoe. The elastic in the outer lining of my spraydeck snapped into place over the edges of my seating hole, and someone handed me my double-ended paddle. Before long, our quintet was on its way.

It was so peaceful and quiet that morning it seemed as if the presence of God was but a wisp away. The sun threaded its way through the tree leaves overhead to embroider the water below, and the hushed splash of water dripped rhythmically off my paddle. A shout disturbed my reverie:

"There's a weir up ahead!"

A weir is composed of two cement walls—one that's set internally against the course of a river and one that presses in from the side. The idea behind it is to control the water's flow. We would travel over the dam with the overflow of the river and ride the heights of its cascade to the smoothness below.

I had not spent the required time in the local swimming pool practicing how to capsize, so to protect myself from unintentionally practicing that day, I watched the others go down the weir before me to see how they handled their canoes. The spectator's spot was in the shade, and I back-paddled gently so as not to get sucked down by the rushing current.

Each girl seemed to pour down the weir like melted butter, which increased my faith in my own ability to make it through.

"Okay, your turn," I heard from below.

I don't quite remember exactly what happened next, but my sketchy memory seems to recall my canoe turning rapidly around to take the weir backwards. Alarm shot adrenaline into my arms, and I frantically used it to my disadvantage enough to catch a spectacular, long-term, eyeball view of the riverbed at the base of the weir.

Canoe paddle now drifting delightedly free of the idiot's grip down the floating waterway . . . body frantically heaving all its strength up and left to get head above water . . . lungs feeling as if there will soon be no air left in them . . . head leaving the suffocating water to gasp in some air, to then plummet again to the river bed . . . screaming out a silent HELP! Prayer inside . . . brain not thinking or connecting at all with the thought of pulling the spraydeck off with the easy-pull cord . . .

Until somehow, suddenly, I was free.

My body slid out of my temporary prison to rise to the surface. Blinking through the drops of water, I saw one of the girls stop her paddling against the current; relief drenching her face.

I sat in silence on the way home—a small bundle of wetness—mulling over the morning's events. Occasionally, the girl who had tried to save me turned to me to reassure herself that I was okay. I, in turn, focused on the fact that I had never pulled the cord of the spraydeck that held me hostage. Deep inside I knew that God had everything to do with my salvation.

On that day, just like He had the evening I knelt by my bed and handed over my sin, God sent me an angelic lifeguard.

And He saved my life.

For the Son of Man came to seek and to save what was lost.

(Luke 19:10)

—Sally Hanan

FAITH UNDER FIRE

Having lived through the Great Depression, my grandmother did not waste any amount of food, no matter how small. Two bites of JELL-O, a spoonful of green beans—every morsel was stored in the refrigerator and served again at the next meal. When food finally became too old to serve again, she fed it to the chickens.

When we sat down for lunch that day, most of the dozen or so dishes on the table looked familiar. Absorbed in searching out the last bit of macaroni and cheese from dinner the night before, I barely heard the phone ring or my grandfather answer it.

What I did hear was the tension in his voice, "Rosie, get the girls. Get in the car! Now! There's a fire!" A fire in any circumstance is dangerous, but when you live in the middle of an oil field, it's life and death.

In the early 1960s my grandfather worked for an oil company, manually recording the oil production of operating wells. My cousin and I spent a two-week vacation there together every summer, deep in the piney woods of East Texas. We were six years old the summer of the fire.

"Hurry, girls, get in the car. Now!" I had never seen my grandmother so frightened. She actually left food on the table without putting anything away as she pushed us out the door. My cousin and I raced to the car. My grandmother jumped into the driver's seat.

"Where's Paw-Paw?" I asked.

"He has to go with the other men to try to put out the fire," my grandmother said. I looked over to see my grandfather hurrying to the faded green pick-up the oil company provided for him to drive.

"Where are we going?" my cousin asked.

"As far away as we can get." My grandmother shoved the gearshift into drive and hit the accelerator.

As we raced down the blacktopped roads, heading for the nearest town, I heard my grandmother do something I had never heard any adult do who wasn't standing in a pulpit. She prayed right out loud.

Lord, please save us. Please save Paw-Paw. Please put out the fire and don't let it spread, she pleaded. Then she commanded the two of us in the back seat, "Pray, girls. Pray for your Paw-Paw and for all the other men."

I don't know which stunned me more—the fire, the escape, or my grandmother praying in normal, conversational words, as if God were riding along, holding our hands and sharing our anxiety. Then my cousin startled me even more. Right there in the backseat floorboard, she got down on her knees, folded her hands, closed her eyes, and prayed right out loud too. I sat speechless, embarrassed at my lack of faith or words.

The rest of that day is a blur. I don't remember where we drove to or how we became aware that the fire was contained and all was safe, including my grandfather. When we returned home, the food was still on the table. None of those details have stayed with me over the years; just my grandmother's faith that God was not far away; He was waiting and listening. He was real, up-close, and personal, and He answered the prayers of a desperate wife and her small granddaughter. I feast on that truth every day.

Therefore let everyone who is godly pray to you while you may be found.

(Psalm 32:6a)

—*Sally Clark*

MYSTERIOUS RESCUE

When I was fourteen years old, I had an experience that could not be explained logically. At the time, I didn't know how to pray, but I like to think my miracle was the result of God's promise in Isaiah 65:24: "Before they call I will answer; while they are still speaking I will hear."

My mother died when I was nine, so I went to live with a foster family. After school I often went to help a lady in the little variety store she owned. I always looked forward to spending time there. The woman was very kind and helped fill the void in my life.

From time to time, her son, Fred, stopped in to take care of an errand for his mother or just visit. He was about twice my age, but spoke and treated me with respect. If I was arranging the jewelry counter, he would take notice of the display, point out a piece, and say, "Pretty, isn't it?"

One day Fred came by the house where I lived. "My mother's very ill, and she asked me to take you to her," he said.

"I'll be ready in a minute. Let me grab my coat and purse." I wanted to help the woman who meant so much to me. "I hope she will be all right."

Fred started the car as he said, "I'm sure she will be." But his voice seemed to lack concern. He sounded almost lighthearted. His attitude confused me, but I kept silent.

It wasn't long until I noticed we missed the turn. "You're not going in the right direction," I said as my uneasiness mounted.

"No," he said, "My mother isn't sick. I have a different plan in mind for you." He flashed a sickening smile in my direction.

My heart pounded and fear gripped me. "Take me home right now!" I shouted.

He laughed, "Don't fight it. You're mine. Think of it—I can give you money, jewelry, anything you want." He drove with one hand and grabbed my arm with his other, pulling me closer. We argued. With every advance, I grew stronger. I pushed him, dug my fingernails into his flesh, and clobbered him with my purse. He stopped the car.

The expression on his face changed. It hardened. "All right," he said, "If you want to be difficult, I have something that might change your mind." Reaching behind the seat, he pulled out a gun.

At that moment, a strange peace surrounded me. I saw nothing, but felt a protective presence. I said in a quiet, confident voice, "You cannot harm me because the Lord is in this car."

Stunned, he backed off. He got out of the car and ran through the trees. I sat there shaking and horrified at this turn of events. I don't know how much time passed before I heard a voice. It was Fred's older brother.

Opening the door he said, "I'm so sorry." He repeated it over and over again. "I can't understand how Fred could do this."

He begged me not to tell his mother, and I agreed. I didn't want to hurt the woman who had been like a mother to me.

"I'll deal with Fred," he promised. "He will never bother you again."

I don't know what happened between the two of them, but I never saw Fred again. By the time I heard the good news of the gospel, my heart was prepared to receive Jesus Christ as my Savior. Any time my faith is tested, I need only remember how God protected me—even before I began to serve Him.

> You are my hiding place; you will protect me from trouble and surround me with songs of deliverance.
>
> (Psalm 32:7)

—Ann Denton as told to Esther M. Bailey

COMFORT FOR A GRANDMOTHER'S HEART

As I waited in the large, crowded airport with my granddaughter, Amanda, by my side, I prayed for safety yet again. Although Amanda was twelve and had flown before, this would be her first flight alone.

She had flown with her mother and sister to visit us but had remained to spend a month after they returned home. I felt uneasy about her flying alone and approached the airline counter to voice my concern. The woman at the counter seemed unconcerned. "Just have her come up to one of us when she reaches her stop-over," she said.

"Okay," I replied, not at all happy with her response. I thought the airline would reassure me that they would look after my granddaughter and make sure she made her next flight. I could imagine her walking around the huge airport alone or rushing to catch her connecting flight and missing it. No telling who would spot her and what they would tell her.

I walked back to my seat next to Amanda and repeated the instruction, hoping I didn't convey my anxiety. I wondered if I should try to find someone on the same flight and ask for their help. But who? Amanda sat and sketched as I waited with her, wondering what would happen.

I prayed again. *Lord, let Amanda find someone to keep track of her for me. Please help her with her next connection.* I looked up from my prayer to see Amanda jump up from her seat and rush to the side aisle where travelers would be disembarking. *What's the attraction?*

Then I saw Amanda sitting on the floor petting a little white terrier. The owner sat with the dog's small zipper case and a bowl of water perched on a cloth pad in front of her. Amanda smiled and talked to the lady excitedly. I got up and walked over to investigate more closely. When I reached the spot, Amanda had the dog in her lap. "I'm dog sitting," she stated proudly. "The owner went to get a coke."

"Oh," I said, thinking this lady must judge character well to leave her little pampered pooch with my granddaughter. I noticed an older woman standing in the aisle holding her boarding pass.

"I'm boarding early," she said, showing me her marked pass.

"My granddaughter is flying alone and she needs to board early too," I replied. The airline officials hadn't told me that, but I knew that's what I would have told a young girl flying alone if it were my airline.

The woman said, "Good. She can stick by me, and we can board together. I'll look out for her." Instantly my apprehension drained away. This was just what I had prayed. I had asked God to provide someone who would take an interest in Amanda to see that she would be okay on the flight. The little dog had drawn her to the place we needed to be to meet the senior citizen. God was good.

I watched as early boarders were called and gave Amanda one last hug before she followed the lady down the aisle, out of sight. I left thanking God for providing someone I felt would connect with Amanda.

Her mother had told her to walk to the baggage claim area when she arrived at her final destination, and she would meet her there. I didn't feel comfortable about that aspect, but I knew that a faithful God who provided help on this end would also provide what Amanda needed to find her place at the end of her flight. I could hardly wait to call but allowed time for her connection and arrival.

Hours later, when I dialed my daughter's cell phone, Amanda answered. "Where are you?" I asked.

A joyful voice said, "I'm riding in the car with Mom!"

"How was your flight?" I asked.

"Oh, fine. I sat by the old lady."

"What about finding your next connection? Did you have to ride in the cart to make it on time?"

She almost laughed. "No, that gate was just across from where I got off the first plane." I smiled and blew kisses back at God. He had made her first flight alone better than I could have designed. All was well. God had been behind the scenes all along, making things work on our behalf.

Thou has dealt well with thy servant, O Lord, according unto thy word.

(Psalm 119:65 KJV)

—*Grace Booth*

Prayer Nugget

Fear and anxious moments are a part of life. When those times occur, they stifle your thought processes and paralyze your mind. But God is sovereign and omnipresent. He knows and sees everything that concerns you. Develop a deep and abiding relationship with Him through reading His Word. Make Him the first one you run to during these times.

Lord Jesus, root me and ground me in Your Word so the world may see You in me during fearful times. In Jesus' name I pray. Amen.

_____

_____

_____

_____

_____

_____

_____

_____

_____

_____

_____

_____

_____

_____

_____

_____

_____

_____

Chapter 3

HEY! I'VE KNOWN YOU FOREVER

⟶⁂☉

EXTRAORDINARY MIRACLES; EVERYDAY FAITH

ONE SUNDAY AFTERNOON during the summer of 2008, my husband and I agreed to take two extra foster children into our home on a pre-adoptive placement. The previous year we had adopted our teenage son through foster care and saw God's hand of provision in that process, but taking two more was a leap of faith.

The children's needs were intense enough that I quit my job as a preschool teacher to stay home and help them adjust to a new family. Not long after, my husband's hours of employment were cut in half. Our budget for groceries shrank in spite of the fact we had two more mouths to feed. Convinced that God had called us to this ministry, we prayed for His miraculous help. After creating a menu and a shopping list, we headed to the store with the available funds. We needed at least $60.00 more than we had.

When the children and I arrived at the store, we resembled a small class on school field trip. I explained the purpose of grocery lists and budgets in hopes they might learn money management skills. Then I lectured about good foods and bad foods, excessive sugars and natural sugars. I took my role as their main teacher and mom seriously, but I knew it would be difficult to purchase healthy foods on the allotted budget. Besides, an inner urge to spoil them with love and goodies tugged at my heartstrings.

Into the cart went some produce, a few packages of pasta, several cans of veggies and soups, some peanut butter and low-sugar jelly, bread, one box of cereal, and miscellaneous paper goods. I punched the numbers into a calculator as I walked through the store, praying and looking at the list. Meat. That's all we still needed in our cart, but we didn't have much money left. We'd have enough to eat, but barely, and nothing to buy anything extra. I prayed I would have enough to get everything on the list we needed.

Father, You own it all, and these are Your children. What should I do?

"Can we buy a frozen pizza?" asked the littlest one, with her index finger twirling in her hair.

"Or maybe some chicken nuggets?" asked her older brother, "Please, please?"

My son had learned in his year with us that begging was not allowed. He stood statue-like, his eyes blinking as fast as windshield wipers.

"Children, we need to buy the things on the list first, but let's pray and see what God wants us to have." I forced a smile. We bowed our heads and asked God to provide. I had already prayed without ceasing since we arrived, but I wanted them to learn about prayer. I opened the large freezer door and scanned the selection. *Wow! What can we afford?*

"Ma'am!" a voice bellowed.

I turned to see a tall, white-haired man with copper skin. He emerged from around the corner after we finished the prayer, but we had said nothing aloud. He reached out his hand toward me.

"Here. God told me to give this to you. I've raised a large family—six children to be exact, and I know what it's like to try and buy groceries. The Lord told me you needed this." He stuffed something into my hand.

"Thank you so much, but how did you know?"

"I was standing around the corner a bit, and the Lord spoke to me loud and clear. He said, 'There's a woman in the next aisle that needs to feed her family. Give her the cash you have on hand.' I know the Lord well enough to believe it was truly His voice. He's done things for me through others many times. I hope this helps. And remember, it's not from me anyway. God is your provider."

That said, he turned around and walked away. I could not find him anywhere in the store. In fact, I asked the cashier if she had seen him.

"I haven't seen anyone like the man you described."

I told her the story with teary eyes and trembling hands.

My new children learned firsthand what prayer and faith mean. My husband and I took a leap of faith to take them in, and God supplied what we needed to care for them.

Then I remembered the gift. In my fist was the crinkled wad of money. I counted the bills. Twenty, forty, sixty—the exact amount of our prayer request! As we completed our shopping trip, the children giggled, and I alternated between laughter and tears. We purchased everything on our list, plus a treat for each child.

My worries ended about how our needs and those of our children would be met. I remembered a verse that my parents quoted to me when I was a child and they too lived by faith as ministry-minded people.

For you are great and do marvelous deeds; you alone are God.

(Psalm 86:10)

—Rebecca Joie Oakes

THE BLESSING OF MY INFERTILITY

As I approached thirty, I felt as if I no longer knew myself. Seemingly overnight, I made a U-turn in my longstanding decision not to have children.

My life experiences had once hardened me against opening myself up to the pain I associated with family ties—things like growing up in a stress-filled house, being alienated from my father for nearly a decade, and watching my aunt struggle to survive the loss of her son, my beloved cousin, in Vietnam.

Now I wanted children—wanted them desperately—but my body betrayed me. For no discernible reason, pregnancy eluded me. Suddenly, my husband and I were trotting back and forth to doctor appointments, and I was reading every book I could find on the subject of fertility. I couldn't understand why God seemed to lavish babies on people who weren't ready for them, who didn't want them, who couldn't or wouldn't take care of them, and yet tell me no.

My waking hours, as well as my restless dreams, were consumed with the fruitless struggle to produce a baby. I prayed, I cried, I screamed, and yet—nothing. I came to understand what a doctor had said in an interview I read. He said the most incredible desperation he ever saw was in patients facing terminal cancer or infertility.

I've always been a person who, when faced with an obstacle, starts trying to blast through it. If that won't work, I immediately start looking for a way to go around, climb over, or tunnel under whatever is standing in my path. After just a year of waiting, we turned to adoption. Reluctantly, I let go of wondering how our DNA would reveal itself in the next generation.

I abandoned thoughts of Lucy Ricardo in her maternity smock and Ricky singing, "We're having a baby, my baby and me." I would have no delivery stories to share when I visited with other women in the coming decades. No Lamaze class or breastfeeding. Instead, we'd be meeting a little stranger and watching to see who he or she would become through the years. We would try to answer questions about the child's birth family and how he or she had come to be our child.

We didn't know it, but a door had just opened to the greatest adventure of our lives—though for more than a year we experienced more struggle and disappointment, more hoops to jump through, and more mountains to climb. In choosing to adopt internationally, we subjected ourselves to state approval, approval by the foreign country's health and welfare agency, approval by that country's immigration office, and also United States immigration.

We needed police clearance, a licensed social service agency's report, financial records, medical clearance, and original birth and marriage certificates—all in multiple copies that were signed, notarized, translated, and bearing certificates of authenticity sealed by the state and federal state departments as well as the foreign government's embassy in the U.S.

At last we got a referral, but it soon fell through. That night, I was walking our dog under a clear, cold sky, consumed with despair. At this point, I felt as if we'd go on this way forever, never reaching our destination, as obstacle after obstacle popped up in our path. As a parent with both birth and adoptive children once said, "Having children by adoption isn't really that different from birth—it's just that the labor you go through to adopt is longer and more painful."

I asked God, *Will we ever get our child?* Suddenly, something occurred that had never happened to me before: a shooting star blazed across the sky, as if in direct answer to my prayer. I cried, knowing something very special was happening.

In 1984, after about a nine-month wait, we finally got a referral of a newborn boy from Honduras. His mother had called him David Antonio—the same first name as my husband, though we would call him Tony. It seemed a divine confirmation that this was indeed our son!

Unbelievably, no new problems emerged, and on a July morning we headed to the airport, lugging our bags, a separate suitcase full of baby supplies, a duffel full of diapers, and another bag of supplies for the Honduran orphanage. As we passed other cars, I thought that on an ordinary day we would have been on our way to work too.

When we arrived in the capital city, Tegucigalpa, many hours later, we were both exhausted and half-sick with nerves. Still, as the cab wove its way to our hotel, I fell in love. The city was poor and not even clean, but full of beautiful brown faces, vivid green banana trees, heaps of fragrant pineapple and fresh flowers, red rooftops, and churches that looked like fantastic wedding cakes. I had studied classroom Spanish since elementary school, and now I was grateful. My heart had acquired a second home.

The next morning, after a short appearance before a court clerk, we received our son, and our lives were transformed. In fact, *we* were transformed. I was suddenly a mother. Instead of the pale, bald, rashy sort of infant I had been, I had a beautiful son with warm brown skin and a full head of dark hair. We bonded quickly, and I realized why God had been saying no and not yet to me. The thought of having another child and missing Tony took my breath away. I knew he had always been intended to be mine.

When we talked to our lawyer, we learned Tony had an older brother and sister who had been adopted by an American couple from another state. We looked them up when we got home, and our extended family grew to include them as well. We had become rich in adopted relatives. Since then, we've gotten together from time to time and shared the joy of celebrating weddings and births.

Two years later we were back in Honduras to adopt our daughter, Francisca. Tony was unable to pronounce her name and christened her *Kika*. She was born just one year and a day after Tony. While we were in Tegucigalpa this second time, Tony's birthmother surprised us with a stroke of incredible timing. She gave birth to a daughter she was unable to care for, and she offered her to us so she and Tony could grow up together. We named her Maria. Suddenly, I was mother to three!

As I had been with Tony, I was overwhelmed with gratitude for my children. If we'd gotten pregnant, or if other referrals had happened sooner, we would have missed our appointment with destiny. As my children grew, they constantly amazed me. They were so beautiful—like the swan raised by ducks—certainly better looking than we were! And they had gifts we couldn't have given them—mechanical aptitude, near-perfect pitch, sewing, photography, music, sculpture.

They gave me gifts, as well—the chance to be a room mother, the enjoyment of their friends, a reason to sit at the school concert or the Christmas pageant with tears in my eyes, a stint as youth group advisor and band chaperone, sleepless nights with a feverish bundle in my arms, or just waiting for the phone to ring when they were out with the car. I experienced the long talks at the kitchen table and going on college tours. They gave me gray hairs, a depleted bank account, and a reason to care about the future. These are ordinary things that I guess most people expect as a matter of course, but the blessing of infertility taught me how precious they really are.

> O Lord, how manifold are thy works! in wisdom hast thou made them all: the earth is full of thy riches.
>
> (Psalm 104:24 KJV)

—*Susan Kimmel Wright*

WAITING FOR OUR MIRACLE

When I was a boy, my mother had a small plaque that hung in the kitchen of our tiny apartment. It read, "Even miracles take a little time."

My wife, Vickie, and I had planned on being the typical American couple. We'd get married, work for a couple of years to earn some stability and get to know one another, and then start our family. We had seen our friends follow this same agenda, and it seemed simple enough.

We learned it is not always so simple.

We went through years of self-doubt, frustration, and bittersweet smiles as we held the newborn babies of our closest friends and agonized over the empty place in our home and hearts. It was frustrating not being able to give each other the baby we wanted so badly, and we longed to be the parents we knew God had made us to be.

After a decade of trying, and having reached the ripe-old age of thirty-eight, we realized that having a baby wasn't going to happen the "old-fashioned way."

Vickie said to me, "Perry, let's investigate other sources for help."

We did. Only to find help is expensive. Help is very expensive.

The process of IVF (in-vitro fertilization) and a subsequent pregnancy and birth would cost tens of thousands of dollars. We had three hundred dollars in the bank. It was a long night at the dinner table. There was anger, and there were tears.

"How could God put such a burning desire, such a lifelong goal to be parents, in our hearts, and then make it impossible to achieve?" Vickie asked.

We didn't have tens of thousands of dollars; we didn't have one thousand dollars. But we did have our house.

Years of scrimping and saving, driving clunker cars, and eating brown-bag lunches had allowed us to pay off our school debts and save just enough for a down payment on a beautiful little three-bedroom, two-bath house on the outskirts of town.

We had both worked full time, living in tiny apartments in bad neighborhoods to save money, crunching numbers until they squeaked, and jumping through every hoop imaginable for ten years to buy that house. It wasn't much, but it was ours. For a kid who'd never lived anywhere but apartment complexes, it was everything. It was a place to have friends over, to plant our own flowers, and to paint the walls whatever shade of purple we pleased; a place of our own. It had been like a dream come true three years earlier when we'd signed papers and moved in. Now it was being made clear to us: we could have our baby if we gave up our home.

The market was ripe, and our agent assured us we could get our asking price, which would leave us just enough to pay off our loan, our few remaining debts, and complete the IVF process one time.

We talked. We argued. We cried.

Most of all, we prayed.

That's when we realized that everything we had scrimped and saved and sacrificed for had been leading to this moment. We weren't being forced out of our home; we were being given an opportunity to have the child we'd always wanted.

All we had to do was sign. And we did.

More sacrifices were made, possessions were sold, and more tears were shed when we stood in the living room of yet another, tiny two-bedroom apartment. Then came the innumerable trips to the doctor, the embarrassing medical tests, the extremely candid conversations with nurses, and the months of limbo, hope, and heartbreak.

During the IVF appointment, only four viable eggs were found. On the morning of implantation, only one had survived. Our doctor put it to us straight. "The odds are against you, but you're here anyway, if you want to give it a try."

We couldn't afford another treatment. We needed a miracle. We said we wanted to try.

It's been three years since we sold our dream house, and our daughter, Grace, just turned one. Nothing was easy about her addition to our family, but she has brought light to our lives that no windows could, and colors to our world that no flowers can ever match. She's our miracle baby.

When Gracie smiles, laughs, and hugs our necks, we know that sometimes miracles take a little time. And our miracle was worth the wait.

O give thanks unto the Lord; call upon his name: make known his deeds among the people.

(Psalm 105:1 KJV)

—Perry Perkins

THE MYSTERIOUS BLONDE

The tall, slender, young blonde wiped her eyes as she hurried past the narrow window that adjoined the office door. Shielded by the upturned collar of her jacket, the brief glimpse of her profile left her identity a mystery. The last and only door past the entrance to our office was the private entry used by Dr. Fox, whose office occupied the end space on the ninth floor of the high-rise medical center. My eyes scanned the appointment book. It offered no clue. The incident sparked my curiosity. *It must be a distraught patient who didn't want to be seen visiting a psychiatrist's office,* I thought.

The ring of the telephone in our small apartment earlier that April morning had interrupted my devotional time.

"Hello?"

"Jeanette. Twilah. Chris needs to take the day off, and I need your help. Could you fill in for her today?"

After a quick glance at my schedule, I said, "Sure. See you at nine." The round clock on the kitchen wall read 7:00 A.M.—time enough to wrap up my devotionals, scarf down breakfast, and dash through my morning routine.

The scenic drive offered a visual drink of springtime in Tulsa. Manicured lawns and gardens laden with colorful azaleas dazzled the landscapes with vibrant blossoms. Tulips and narcissus craned their heads skyward in splashes of vivid color. I imagined the Master Gardner had fashioned this previewed glimpse of heaven just for me.

The medical building that housed Twilah's office sat on a hilltop overlooking the city. I parked my car, walked through the entry doors, slipped into the elevator, and pressed nine. The polished, rich mahogany panel reflected the faces of its passengers. I leaned against it as the carriage moved effortlessly upward without a ripple. A gentle slowing, the doors opened, and I stepped into the hall.

Keys in hand, I turned the lock on the office door and stepped inside. One glance around identified the first task of the day. Magazines were scattered here and there, gum wrappers, stale coffee cups—neat up the waiting room. De-cluttering finished, I made a fresh pot of coffee and inserted *Vivaldi's Four Seasons* CD into the Bosch system.

The door to her inner office opened and she craned her neck around the corner, "Hi," she said. "The coffee smells wonderful. I had some at the house, but the aroma makes me want another cup."

"One cup just the way you like it coming right up."

"Any messages?"

"The answering service received three calls during the night. I'll bring the messages in with your coffee."

After I placed the messages and coffee on her desk, I greeted her with a hug. She studied the call list and said, "I need to return these. When the first patient arrives, ask him to be seated for a few minutes. I'll buzz you when I'm ready."

"Good morning, Mr. Simmons. Dr. Fox will be with you shortly. Would you care for some coffee?"

The morning flew by with the patients' arrivals and departures pretty much on schedule. I stayed busy. By noon, my stomach's audible gurgles were embarrassing. The door to her office remained closed. We usually left the office for lunch, but today something was different. I waited.

That's when I caught a glimpse of the mysterious young blonde as she hurried past the narrow window. Her clandestine visit with Dr. Fox must be from one of the messages left with the answering service. The young woman chose anonymity.

As I mulled over the mystery, the office door opened and Twilah walked toward the front desk, purse in hand. "Let's run over to the Bistro for lunch."

"Sounds good to me." I did not mention the mysterious caller.

After lunch we returned to the office, and the afternoon whizzed by much like the morning. We closed the office on Tuesdays at 3:00 P.M. due to the evening Bible study Dr. Fox led. It allowed her to avoid evening traffic, have dinner, and hone her thoughts before she left for the meeting. It helped me too, because I attended the study and liked to arrive early for a front-row seat.

That evening I was unavoidably late. The sounds of the praise and worship music greeted me in the parking lot. Too late for a front-row seat, I slipped into a chair near the back of the room and joined in the singing. As the music ended, I glanced around the room at the sea of faces. That's when I saw Kathy Monroe holding a newborn baby. It took me by surprise, because the Monroes had no children.

They were newcomers to the Bible study, and while I had not met them, I knew who they were. They owned a large furniture store, and their television ads frequented the airwaves. Rick's tall frame, dark hair, and olive complexion contrasted with Kathy's soft blue eyes, fair skin tones, and porcelain-like features. They were a striking couple.

I scanned the rest of the crowd to see who else was in attendance but gave Kathy and her baby another glance. This time when I looked at her, I was completely baffled. There was no baby! What happened? It made no sense. Neither she nor Rick held a baby, and I knew I had seen a baby in her arms. I paid little attention to the lesson as I tried to figure out what I knew my eyes had seen. My mind couldn't let go of it. It played and replayed the mysterious experience.

Twilah's concluding, "Amen," recaptured my focus. People stood as they collected their belongings and prepared to leave. Some lingered around Twilah, waiting to speak with her; some chatted with friends as they made their way toward the door. Their departures moved like molasses in winter. I worked my way through the crowd toward Twilah. My strange experience needed answers. When I reached her, I said, "Something I can't explain happened to me tonight. I saw Kathy Monroe holding a newborn baby in her arms."

Without hesitation she said, "She needs to hear this! Go and tell her."

I glanced in their direction and saw them standing near their seats preparing to leave. As I approached them, Twilah's counsel encouraged me. Not having been formerly introduced, I extended my hand and said, "Hi, I don't believe we've met. I'm Jeanette Sharp, Dr. Fox's sister." Their warm response eased the awkwardness I felt inside. "Kathy, during tonight's meeting, I had a strange experience. I saw you holding a newborn baby." Her hand flew to her mouth as tears filled her eyes. She looked from me to Rick. The glow on their faces spoke volumes.

Twilah made her way toward us, smiling. "Did you tell?"

"Yes."

"Kathy, I would like to share the full story with Jeanette, if that's okay?"

Kathy nodded.

"This morning, Kathy came to see me just before lunch. She's had several miscarriages in the past and is pregnant again. Yesterday, she began to show symptoms of losing this baby too. Today I prayed with her for a full-term delivery of a healthy baby."

"So you're the mystery woman I saw hurry past the office window this morning!"

They left that evening with a new peace in their hearts and the confident assurance their prayers would be answered.

During my drive home, I pondered all that had happened with an expanded sense of awe and wonder of God's greatness. Seven months later, Kathy gave birth to a healthy baby boy, just as the Lord had shown me.

My frame was not hidden from you when I was made in the secret place. When I was woven together in the depths of the earth, your eyes saw my unformed body.

(Psalm 139:15-16a)

I will pour out my Spirit on all people. Your sons and daughters will prophesy, your old men will dream dreams, your young men will see visions. Even on my servants, both men and women, I will pour out my Spirit in those days.

(Joel 2:28-29)

—Jeanette Sharp

FASHIONABLY MATERNAL

"I have nothing to wear," I complained out loud as I searched through my tiny closet. Five months into my first pregnancy I was running out of things that would fit over my expanding waistline. Going shopping for cute maternity outfits to make me look blissfully pregnant and fashionably maternal was not an option. My husband and I were in missionary training and had very little income, definitely not enough income to purchase a new wardrobe.

I had been praying about the things I needed—including maternity outfits—because of the coming baby, but so far I hadn't seen an answer. *Lord,* I prayed again as I rummaged through dresses and tops, *I don't have much that fits me anymore. What am I supposed to do?*

"Don't worry," seemed to be the answer as I recalled Jesus' instruction.

But I *was* worried. Just a few more inches of growth and I wouldn't have anything that fit. For the present, I needed to find something to wear. I had guests arriving soon to spend the weekend. Two friends who had been in a Bible study group with us in Indiana were driving to Pennsylvania to visit us.

I didn't want to look like a poor missionary when they arrived, but I didn't have much choice in what to wear. I grabbed the roomiest thing in my closet and slipped it on. It took a bit of tugging to get it to fit around my tummy. I tied a colorful scarf around my neck and hoped it would draw attention away from my growing belly and make me look more fashionable.

Just as I finished tying my scarf, there was a knock at our apartment door. When my husband and I opened it, our friends Hoyt and Rosemary were standing there with their arms full of packages.

"Congratulations!" they shouted.

"We're delivering a long-distance baby shower," Rosemary added. "Last week, everyone in the group arrived at the Bible study with gifts for your coming little one. There's more in the car."

After we carried in a carload of packages that were wrapped in pink and blue paper, I began to open the gifts. As I unwrapped baby blankets, diapers, booties, and sleepers for "Baby Huddleston," I found several packages marked "For Connie."

"What are these?" I asked.

"Open them and see," Rosemary replied.

I grabbed a large, flat box and peeled off the blue paper. When I lifted the lid and pushed the tissue paper aside, I saw a stylish, baby-blue maternity outfit. "It's just what I need," I said.

"Since this is your first pregnancy, the ladies in the Bible study knew you would need new things to wear," Rosemary said.

When I opened the other packages with my name on them, I found cute tops and stretchy skirts and slacks. As I looked at everything, I knew "will he not much more clothe you?" is true— even for maternity clothes.

. . . See how the lilies of the field grow. They do not labor or spin. Yet I tell you that not even Solomon in all his splendor was dressed like one of these. If that is how God clothes the grass of the field, which is here today and tomorrow is thrown into the fire, will he not much more clothe you, O you of little faith? So do not worry, saying . . . "What shall we wear?"

(Matthew 6:28-31)

—*Connie Alexander Huddleston*

GOD CARES ABOUT THE SMALLEST DETAILS

"It's time."

"It is? When did it start? How far along is she? Is she okay?" I could barely contain the excitement I felt at the reality of becoming a grandmother—and soon.

"We're headed to the hospital now. I'll call you when she gets closer, okay? I'm sure it will be a little while, so try to relax. I'll get back to you later. Gotta go. Love you, Mom."

"I love you . . . " Too late. Chris had already hung up. I looked at my husband. "We're going to be grandparents."

"We already knew that, didn't we?" Keith drew me in for a hug. "Grandma and Grandpa. Has a nice sound to it, doesn't it."

Chris and Jen lived about forty minutes from us. Close enough for us to be the active grandparents we knew we would be. And close enough to reach the hospital before our grandbaby made his or her debut appearance. Twenty-four hours later, the phone rang.

"Pray! And get here as soon as you can. Jen's having an emergency C-section, and things don't look good." Once again, Chris hung up the phone before I was able to get more information from him.

Keith pulled the car around while I called our church to put Jen on the prayer chain. We headed out to pick up our daughter at the high school. Leaving Cassie's car in the school parking lot, the three of us headed to the hospital. We arrived there in record time.

"Jen so wanted a natural birth." Chris looked exhausted. "But it's a good thing we didn't wait. It turned out that the cord was wrapped around the baby's neck. He was suffocating. If we had waited any longer, the baby wouldn't have made it."

"The baby? He's here? It's a boy?"

"Come on, I'll take you to meet your grandson." Chris opened the door and I hurried through, my husband right on my heels. What a sight to behold. Jen was cradling her newborn son. Chris slid in behind us and reached for Devon. *Devon.* He cuddled the sweet bundle in his arms and carried him to me.

"I'm so sorry we weren't here for you." The thought of Chris and Jen being alone in their decision to move ahead with surgery without family support saddened me.

"We weren't alone, Mom." Turned out that for absolutely no reason, my brother Paul, who shared a special bond with Chris, just happened to be in town. And so was my sister-in-law. I don't know how they received word that Jen and Chris were at the hospital, but they showed up at the exact time our son and daughter-in-law needed family support and counsel.

"I guess that hardly surprises me." I snuggled my grandson close. "I asked God to provide whatever you and Jen needed during labor and delivery. Seems He did, didn't He?"

"He did." My son reached over and caressed his son's tiny head.

I reflected on the truth of Psalm 139:14: "I praise you because I am fearfully and wonderfully made; your works are wonderful, I know that full well." How wonderfully God showed His loving care by carefully orchestrating the smallest details regarding the birth of our first grandson, Devon.

—*Carolyn R. Scheidies*

MOM, I'M LOSING HER!

The baby she longed for wasn't due for another seven weeks. Something was dreadfully wrong. Knowing every second could be crucial to the survival of their unborn child, Jami's doctor advised her to go to the nearest emergency room instead of driving to the large city hospital where she had intended to give birth. Jami's husband, Rick, drove to Hugh Chatham Memorial Hospital in their hometown of Elkin, North Carolina.

Jami had suffered an abruption, a condition in which the placenta separates from the uterus, causing internal bleeding. The baby could not survive without the lifeline of the placenta and was drowning in her mother's blood. The diagnosis took precious time because Jami didn't exhibit any of the conditions commonly associated with an abruption.

As drugs were administered to put Jami to sleep, she asked God to please keep her baby safe, not realizing the danger she too was in. Jami lost consciousness not knowing what she would awaken to. As the pending gloom of the emergency grew, Rick was asked to leave the operating room. We could hear the medical staff barking orders through the brief opening of the door as he emerged.

Dressed in green scrubs, Rick tearfully dropped to his knees just outside the door. His desperate and unashamed prayer was heard throughout the quiet corridors. *Please God, don't let my wife and little girl die! I know I don't deserve it, but I beg You not to take them from me.*

We marveled at the number of Christians on duty that July night. Maybe someone carried heartache or was discouraged. Maybe someone's faith was weakened and was about to give up on God or a marriage. As the night wore on, God brought into their lives a couple that never intended to be there, a perfect pregnancy that had gone terribly wrong, and a baby that wasn't ready to be born.

The threat of broken hearts loomed heavily upon us. What if God's will was not our will? The thought of watching Rick and Jami go home in grief without Elizabeth in their arms made us nauseous. To think we might never hold our grandchild in our arms was unbearable, but God gave us the strength to pray for His will to be done and to trust Him.

Elizabeth's tiny heart stopped beating before she could be snatched from danger by the emergency cesarean. As our lifeless, three-pound-thirteen-ounce baby lay before the doctor, the staff held their breath in silent prayer. Her father's heart-wrenching prayers pierced the air as he crouched near the closed doors. Jami, protected temporarily by the drug-induced sleep, was unaware her baby had lost the fight for her life. Each second ticked away the hopes and dreams of our families awaiting Elizabeth's birth.

They later said they felt the strong presence of the Lord filling the operating room. The pediatrician, Dr. Walker, skillfully performed resuscitation procedures on Elizabeth. After one minute, which seemed like an eternity, God breathed life into a stillborn infant. God performed a miracle before their very eyes as Elizabeth took her first breath. There was rejoicing in the O.R. A happy Dr. Walker brought Rick the good news. The baby was alive, but they still needed time with Jami. She had lost a lot of blood.

Rick followed a nurse to the small emergency nursery as she ran pushing the incubator that held his newborn daughter.

Brenner Children's Hospital in Winston-Salem, known for its expert neonatal intensive care unit, had been called. Heavy rain had grounded the emergency helicopter, but a team of experts was on the way by ambulance to whisk Elizabeth away.

I will always remember the moment I first saw her. She was so small lying in her plastic enclosure. A clear oxygen tent that looked like the dome of a cake plate was over her head. Surprisingly, she was awake and moving around. I had imagined her lying motionless with purplish skin. Oh, how I longed to touch her! Tears blurred my vision.

Doctor Walker smiled. "Do you want to touch her?"

Laying my hand on my heart, I whispered, "You mean, it's okay?"

He opened the side of her sanitized world. I praised God for the wonderful gift he had bestowed upon us as I carefully stroked the soft, smooth skin of her leg.

Several delivery room staff members crowded in to see the miracle child they had witnessed taking her first breath of life as they prayed. The doctors and nurses repeated the miracle story to us. The birth of Elizabeth would bond them forever. Doctor Walker patted Rick on the shoulder saying, "It was your prayers that did it. We could hear you."

The staff from Brenner Children's Hospital arrived and began preparing Elizabeth for the forty-five minute trip.

Our concern for Jami grew as we waited in her room. Had something happened to her? What was taking so long? The Brenner staff would be taking the baby soon, and we feared they would leave before Jami could see Elizabeth. She would be brokenhearted.

Finally, our badly swollen and exhausted daughter was wheeled in. As her bed was placed under gadgets attached to the wall, she reached for Rick's hand. "Is our baby really okay?"

He assured her with a smile. "Yes, she is."

It was like royalty was arriving when our little princess was rolled into the room, followed by the staff, along with the Brenner team. She rested beside her mother's bed. The room became reverently quiet as we witnessed Jami seeing her precious baby and touching her for the first time since becoming two.

A nurse opened the small, round door on the side of the incubator. Jami ached to hold Elizabeth and cuddle her close, but that wasn't possible. As if they both knew what the other needed, Elizabeth stretched her arm out from her side, making her wee hand accessible by the opened door. Jami lovingly touched the velvety skin of Elizabeth's palm. Her tiny fingers hugged her mother's pinky finger. Even though her fragile hand was too small to wrap completely around Jami's finger, she held on as if to say, "I'll be okay, Mommy."

Tears of joy streamed uncontrollably down Jami's cheeks in the hushed room. The tender moment brought tears to family and staff alike. My husband and I, along with Rick's parents, stood in awe of God's love. What a privilege it would be to hold our grandchild to our hearts soon. We were overcome with amazement.

Breaking the silence, an EMT explained to Jami the importance of getting Elizabeth to the neonatal intensive care unit as soon as possible. She spoke of the tests they would be running on her once inside the ambulance, and to brace herself for the baby being hospitalized for approximately three months.

We saw the indescribable pain etched on Jami's face at the thought of being separated from her baby. Realizing the separation must occur for Elizabeth to get the care she desperately needed, Jami reluctantly pulled her finger from the perfect little fist that held on to her. The small, round door was close and latched. Almost as quickly as she came, Elizabeth and her entourage rushed toward the elevator.

Feeling torn between his wife and daughter, Rick pleaded, "Should I go with her? She's all alone. She needs me!"

Jami quickly urged him. "Yes. Go with her, Rick."

"We'll wait for you to get behind us." The ambulance driver said.

Rick kissed Jami goodbye. "I'll be back as soon as I can."

The delivery room nurses lingered to tell the story of the miracle they had witnessed to Jami. Again they talked of how strongly they had felt the presence of God and the severity of the situation for mother and child. Jami wept at hearing of the threat of losing her own life, but especially the life of her baby.

The doctors and nurses agreed often over the next forty-eight hours. "It is only by the grace of God the baby is here."

At Brenner Children's Hospital, Elizabeth was too weak to nurse. A feeding tube was inserted. On the seventh day of her life she was tested for brain damage because of the loss of oxygen during birth. The tests came back showing no apparent brain damage.

One day, the nurse on duty said Elizabeth was lying in bed with one little outstretched hand, reaching toward heaven, as if she was praising the Lord. We thought that was adorable until we learned later that is a sign of distress in preemies. Could it be that even babies reach out to God in their dark days?

After much prayer and only ten days in intensive care, Elizabeth came home in her twelve-inch doll clothes.

> For the Lord God is a sun and shield: the Lord will give grace and glory;
> no good thing will he withhold from them that walk uprightly.
>
> (Psalm 84:11 KJV)

—Aggie Stevenson

PRAYER NUGGET

God's plan for our lives begins long before conception. He knows the number of our days before one of them comes to pass. He confirms His intimate knowledge of us through His Word. The Psalmist said, "All the days ordained for me were written in your book before one of them came to be" (Psalm 139:16).

Father, thank You for Your plan for each and every life. Help me remember that life is a gift from You and is of great worth in Your eyes. In Jesus' name I pray. Amen.

_____

_____

_____

_____

_____

_____

_____

_____

_____

_____

_____

_____

_____

_____

_____

_____

_____

_____

_____

_____

Chapter 4

IT'S ALL IN THE FAMILY

AT THE END OF THE FENCE

DAD WAS NEVER anyone's favorite person. He had been a hard man, and he had sabotaged most of his relationships with his children, daughters-in-law, and grandchildren. Unable to express himself positively, he often offended and caused hurt feelings.

He led a prosperous life and traveled extensively with my mother before she passed away from cancer. Having been dependent on her for so many years, living alone was not an option for him. He soon found companionship with a wonderful woman we all grew to love. She tolerated his harsh ways and was devoted to making his life complete. They lived simply and happily together, and since they were both healthy, were able to enjoy more freedom than some elderly folks.

Time eventually caught up with them, and good health began to fade away. Only a month after his ninetieth birthday celebration, Dad lay dying in a hospital bed. I rushed to his side—leaving my two brothers on alert to come from out of state at a moment's notice. When I arrived, Dad was incoherent and working hard for each breath. He looked so frail and thin; his face was colorless and gaunt. Because he had pneumonia, and there was evidence of a mild heart attack, the doctor told me and his loving companion to prepare for his death. I could hear his lungs rattle as he breathed, and it was very difficult to stand by and do nothing. It just didn't seem right, and I felt helpless. Could the doctor be wrong? Might Dad have a chance?

I stayed with him that night in the hospital room, expecting the worst to happen at any moment. As I kept watch over him, I contemplated the fact that he had not come to a personal knowledge of Jesus. I tried over the years to share my faith with him but had never seen any evidence of a receptive heart. During the night, the nurse, a Christian friend from our previous church, prayed for Dad with me as he slept. Over the next several hours his condition seemed to worsen. Fear gripped my heart as I realized my chances to guide him to his heavenly home might be slipping away. There had to be a way. I couldn't give up on him yet. I couldn't just let him lie there and die, waiting to drown in his own fluids. Looking out the window, I cried out to God. *Lord, You said You would make a way where there is no way.*

Just then Dad began to cough. He struggled to bring up the obstruction choking him. I leaned toward him, putting my face close to his. "Dad, do you think you could cough up that stuff?" I heard him say a weak "Yes." I helped him sit up and encouraged him to spit out everything as he coughed. Grabbing a handful of paper towels, I tried to wipe up everything from inside his mouth. He coughed and coughed, and out came what seemed to be pints of the phlegm that had been rattling around in his chest. There was some blood mixed in with it, but I tried not to show my concern. I had to stay strong and keep myself from becoming queasy at the sight. Dad lay back down, and all at once I sensed something good was about to happen.

After long moments passed, Dad opened his eyes and said, "You know, I feel better!"

It was a shock to see him come alive. He continued to cough up his congestion as I cleaned his mouth with the wet swabs the nurse left by the bed. After a few hours he could carry on a conversation and ask me questions. A miracle had occurred, and I knew it was my time to speak to Dad about the God he had rejected all these years. This could be his last opportunity to choose heaven. He was my dad, and I wanted to see him again someday. I let him rest, knowing he was exhausted from his ordeal. But I knew his life had been spared as an answer to my prayer.

During the night Dad was restless and awake off and on. Pulling out my Bible, I began reading to myself. I looked up to see his eyes open, and I asked him if I could read some scriptures aloud. "That would be fine." After reading for a moment, I decided to be blunt.

"You know, Dad, you need to ask Jesus into your heart, don't you?" I sensed he knew the truth.

"Yes," he said, "I know I've been a hard man." Hearing the words surprised me. He had never admitted to any shortcomings before.

"The Bible says that you only need to believe and call on the name of Jesus and you . . . "

"Shall be saved." He finished my sentence. It was a surprising response, as I had no idea he knew any Scripture. I seized the moment and told him we were going to pray and ask Jesus to come into his heart. As we prayed together, the burden from my own heart lifted. It was such a relief to know that I would be spending eternity with both my parents.

His condition continued to improve, much to the amazement of the doctor. She was truly convinced he would not live through his illness but now told us to make preparations, not for a funeral, but for a care facility. I called my brothers and gave them the good news. They were off their alert status.

In the next few months, Dad lost his beloved companion and moved to a nursing home close to me. His disposition and demeanor changed for the better, and he seemed much happier and content. The nurses at the nursing home all liked him and gave him the attention he loved.

One day, as my wife and I were visiting him at his residence, he asked us if we could see the fence. He pointed down the hallway. "I'm supposed to meet a man at the end of the fence today." My wife and I looked at each other—amused at his little bout of dementia. We continued our conversation, but later he repeated his story about the man at the end of the fence. We left him that day, chuckling and remarking about how good he looked and what a great visit we had with him.

At eight o'clock that evening we received a call. "Come quickly, I think your dad is dying." The nurse was frantic.

We arrived just as the paramedics were leaving. Dad was gone. He had slipped away suddenly without warning. We sat with him for a while, crying in disbelief. On the way home, it dawned on me. He had gone to meet the man at the end of the fence. His Savior had been waiting to receive him, and Dad could see Him. It made perfect sense. Dad had been a farmer all his adult life, and many days were spent walking the fence to check posts or survey the fields of grain. It was no surprise that Jesus would call him there.

There were times in my life that I doubted Dad would ever come to know the Savior. I prayed over the years and waited patiently for an opportunity—an opening into his hardened heart. I can't say I wasn't nervous about running out of time. But I had to trust God.

God is faithful and mighty to save. His mercy and grace will extend to the hardened, the stubborn, the weak, and the doubtful. That was my dad, but time and faith changes everything. Someday I will meet him at the end of the fence, and we will walk the fields again.

> Let us hold fast the profession of our hope without wavering: (for he is faithful that promised;)
>
> (Hebrews 10:23 KJV)

—Jan Cline, as told by my husband, Jerry

DEPARTMENT STORE ANGEL

I rushed through the house mumbling to myself, "I can't do this!"

"Do what?" asked my husband. "What's wrong? Where're you going?"

"I have to run to the store. I was watching television with Mom and noticed it was wet under her chair. I didn't realize at first that she had had an accident, and neither did she. I just helped her shower and put on clean clothes. I'm going to get her some diapers."

"Why did she do that?" he asked.

"I don't know why. I'm at a loss. She can't help what's happening any more than I can. I'm sorry you have to go through this with me, but she's my mom, and I'll do anything and everything I can for her."

With tears coursing toward my chin, I hurried to dress. I had to get to the store and back before Mom needed something else.

"Please keep an eye on Mom. I don't think she'll need anything, but please stay near."

I talked to myself all the way to the store. I couldn't believe I was going to buy diapers. I realized that years ago my mom had diapered me, and now our roles were reversed. I longed for the days we went shopping together. I missed the times we sat and talked for hours about good times and bad. A once very active and productive woman had been turned into a meek, frail, helpless person.

By the time I got to the store, my eyes were red and my face was wet with tears. I prayed as I had many times before. *Dear God, please help me be a better person. Help me have more patience and understanding for Mom. Please show me how to handle this and how to make things better for her.*

This was my first time buying this type of product, and I stood and read each label. What size? What brand? I was so confused and felt helpless. A lady came up to the shelf and quickly took a package. *Wow, she must know what she's doing!*

"Excuse me, but do you know anything about these undergarments? I'm buying this for my mom, she's ninety-five, and it's my first time to buy them. I have no idea what I'm doing."

The woman smiled, "I'm buying these for my mom. She's ninety-two. My mom likes this brand best."

The woman and I began sharing stories about our moms. I explained how being a caregiver was the hardest job I had ever done.

"There are many days I feel like I can't keep doing this job. I love my mom and want the best for her, but so often I fear I'm not doing enough; other times I'm completely overwhelmed with it all. I question if I'm up to the challenge of what lies ahead next."

"Oh, my word! I feel the same way," the woman responded. "I feel so bad for my husband. He's been so wonderful. We have basically put our lives on hold."

"We have too. My husband doesn't complain, but I know it's hard on him. I feel so guilty. We never go anywhere, and if we do, I have to get someone to sit with Mom. I feel like I'm always in a hurry. I can't leave the house for any long length of time."

"I'm so happy I met you," the woman said, offering her hand. "Now I don't feel as if I'm the only one going through this."

"I'm happy to meet you too. I don't get to talk to many people. All my friends have stopped calling since I can't go out and do things with them. I'm not much fun. My life revolves around Mom and her needs."

"I know just how you feel. I have to get back to my mom. I'm just picking up a few supplies on my way back from a doctor's appointment. This is going to sound crazy, but do you have an e-mail address?"

"Yes, I do. I'd love to hear from you. I think we could be a great support system for each other." I searched for a paper to write down my e-mail address.

We shared a few more stories and parted, promising to stay in touch.

I left the store feeling better than I did when I left the house. Just sharing stories made me feel better. I couldn't wait to get home and tell my husband about my new friend.

"Did you find what you were looking for?" my husband asked.

"Yes, I think so. Guess what! I met a wonderful woman in the incontinence aisle. We talked for a long time. She's the caregiver for her mom. The more we talked the more alike we were. We're both going through the same things. We exchanged e-mail addresses. I sure hope she writes to me."

I was so excited, I even told Mom about meeting this wonderful woman.

"See, Mom, a lot of people wear these. It's nothing. It's just like your regular underwear." I wanted to convince her to wear them without feeling embarrassed.

"The lady at the store said her mom has been wearing them for years. I know you don't like the idea, but I think it's for the best. Now you don't have to worry about getting to the bathroom in time. You still have to go to the bathroom, but if you have an accident it won't be so bad."

My mom agreed to give it a try, and that made me feel so much better. The very next day I got an e-mail from my new friend. This was just the beginning of what I knew would be a lifelong friendship.

I feel God answered my prayers and sent me a special friend. In my heart, I like to think of her as my "department store angel."

A man that hath friends must show himself friendly.
(Proverbs 18:24a KJV)

—*Marilyn E. Freeman*

THE FADED, BROWN-LEATHER PURSE

When my mother died, I had the daunting task of going through her belongings. She wasn't rich, and she didn't have much. I just wanted to box everything up and send it to Goodwill.

My mother and I didn't see eye-to-eye. She was an alcoholic, and I gave up on her. I didn't think she was worth much in life or in death, and I was angry with her. I had spent years taking care of *her*. It was supposed to be the other way around, but it never was.

Right before I turned sixteen, my father died. My mother, in her "alcoholic wisdom," decided to uproot us and move three thousand miles away from my father's family. I was angry with her and decided to run away from home. I didn't get the chance, and we made peace, but not for long.

Throughout my adulthood, my mother drank. She wasn't a happy drunk. She was a mean drunk, and I suffered horribly from her anger. I stopped speaking to her and even made her leave my home. After all, I had my own family to think about.

Over the next two years, I prayed daily that somehow she and I would reconcile.

The phone call came two years after I had ejected her from my life. It was my aunt.

"Debra?"

"Yes."

"Your mom's in the hospital. She's dying."

When I got to the hospital, Mother was in a coma. I didn't get to tell her I was sorry for the things I had done or the anger I had held against her. She died not knowing I forgave her.

I packed her clothes with care and placed them in the box for the thrift store. Her pictures were carefully laid in a box to bring home. At the bottom of the junk pile, I spotted it. Her old, faded, brown-leather purse. Fond memories flooded my mind. Memories of the times before the drinking began.

She used to keep the purse inside her dress, next to her heart. I always wondered why she did that. I thought it was because she didn't want anyone to take her money. But I found out that day she kept it next to her heart for one reason.

Tucked inside the old, faded, leather purse were a few old coins and a picture of me. Tears washed down my cheeks as I turned the picture over and saw the date. I was three. My mother did love me! She carried me next to her heart for thirty-three years, until her death.

God did answer my prayers—but in His timing.

I'm thankful for the warm memories of her I hold in my heart. I'm even thankful for the not-so-great memories. We shared a lifetime of love and sorrow that made us who we became. I love you, Mom!

In the morning, O Lord, you hear my voice; in the morning I lay my requests before you and wait in expectation.

(Psalm 5:3)

—*Debra Elliott*

RESTORED RELATIONSHIP

I was reading about the Holy Spirit's role in the life of a Christian when the thought struck me. Not a new thought, because on several occasions my husband, Ray, had said, "You should go see your dad." My inclination to act on his advice *was* something new.

The thirty-year separation between my father and me started out as a natural consequence of circumstances. As a teenager, I actually welcomed my parent's divorce, because the friction between them had disturbed me for years. Each of them had good qualities as individuals, but together they made a sorry team.

Even though I'd been close to my dad as a little girl, I was content to keep an arm's-length relationship with him after the divorce. Life with my mother went smoother that way.

Dad remarried and moved to another state. By the time he and Gladys returned to Ohio, I was ready to leave my hometown. On return visits, it never occurred to me to look up my father. I knew it would upset my mother, and I believed Dad was happy with his new family and didn't need me.

That concept held through the years. So it surprised me that as I read about the Holy Spirit, my mind turned toward Dad. Was I supposed to get in touch with him?

Ray and I had already planned a trip that would take us from Arizona to Ohio. Our June arrival would be close enough to be considered a Father's Day celebration. My mother had died the year before, and I had nearly recovered from the trauma connected with her long illness.

I've never been quick to proclaim a revelation from God; some of my impressions had been wrong in the past. The suggested prayer I read resolved any lingering doubts. *Lord, what shall I do now? Shall I dial that telephone number? Tell me the first step. I don't even know where my father lives.*

As it turned out, the first step wasn't up to me. A few days later, I was shocked to receive a letter from Aunt Kate, my dad's sister. How did she even get my address? There had been no communication with the family since my parents' divorce. She still lived in Ohio, not far from Dad. She wanted me to come see her.

The uncertainty of our arrival in Ohio prompted me to write Aunt Kate that we'd get in touch before we arrived. For three days her phone was either busy or there was no answer. I began to question if God was leading, but Ray said, "We'll just go to Ohio and look her up."

Even after reliving old memories with Aunt Kate, I felt strange about contacting Dad. My husband gave me an encouraging nudge.

The time had come for me to make the phone call. I didn't know what to say, so once again I leaned on Ray. He helped me work up an approach that gave me confidence as I dialed the number.

"Is this Mr. Litt?" I asked when a male voice answered.

"Yes."

"My name is Esther Bailey; it used to be Esther Litt. Do you remember me?"

"No." I wondered what had gone wrong.

"Is this Emmer Litt?" I fumbled.

"No, this is his son, Steve." I started to speak, but before I did, his words tumbled out. "Are you my sister?"

Steve and I hit it off from the start. Later, as he led me to our father, he said, "This is your dad."

The awkward moment I had anticipated vanished when I met the stranger who had meant so much to me as a child. In fact, he wasn't a stranger at all. He was still my dad. To avoid a display of sentimentality, he clapped his feet at the same time he clapped his hands. I remembered he always did have his own special brand of humor.

My visit, he said, played out his dream of three nights earlier. As he described our meeting in the dream, I was glad I came.

The whole time I contemplated seeing my father, I wondered about his relationship with the Lord. My mother became a Christian several years after their marriage. Her conversion brought many good results, but compatibility with my father wasn't one of them. The more she developed spiritually, the more my father chose the opposite direction. That had all changed for Dad. He quoted scripture and spoke of eternal life with the Lord.

We heard the love story between my dad and Gladys—their meeting that almost didn't happen. It seemed to be a marriage made in heaven. Gladys, the woman who had devoted her life to making Dad happy, hugged me and said, "I love you."

As we left that day, Dad stood by the screen door and said, "I'll pray for you." The restoration of our relationship was slow in coming and brief in duration. Without the prompting of the Holy Spirit, it wouldn't have happened at all.

A longing fulfilled is sweet to the soul.

(Proverbs 13:19a)

—Esther M. Bailey

From Praise to Paradise

Hot tears threatened to spill over. I laid my forehead against the airplane window and pressed tissue to my eyes before they fell. I knew within a few weeks Mom would go home, not from the hospital to her earthly home in Texas, but to her eternal home. I don't know how I managed to find the strength to walk out of her room that day, but I did. I thought of our precious last days together. We read the Bible, sang old hymns, and watched our favorite movies.

I'll never forget.

The plane touched down at the Oakland airport in California, and I immediately learned that my three-year-old grandson, Luke, had been rushed to the hospital for emergency surgery due to an obstructed bowel. Powerless to change his circumstances, I prayed. It was the only—and best—thing I could do for him.

I called Mama and told her about Luke. "I wish I could hold him," she said. "I wish I could do something, but I can't even help myself." I understood the frustration in her voice. She had been an active, independent woman until now.

"Luke could really use your prayers, Mama." The familiar sting of tears once again obscured my vision. "He needs a miracle."

"I can pray," she said. "And I will pray." I pictured my frail mother lying in her hospital bed, trapped in her helplessness. She could have merely given in to her despair, but instead she prayed for her great-grandson.

Over the next few weeks, Mama and I resisted the temptation to worry, and we continued praying. We spoke frequently by phone, reminding one another of James 5:15: "And the prayer offered in faith will make the sick person well; the Lord will raise him up." When the doctors finally released Luke, I couldn't wait to tell Mama.

"Praise God! Hallelujah!" Her voice burst through the phone, and I pulled the receiver away from my ear. She may have been physically weak, but she was spiritually mighty and strong.

Mama's last task on this earth was prayer for her great-grandson. The morning following her thanksgiving prayer, a nurse found Mama sitting up in the bed with her legs hanging off the side, something she had not done since arriving at the hospital. The nurse told me she asked my mother what she was doing.

My mother responded, "Just dangling my feet."

I believe her earthly cares, pain, and suffering vanished at that very moment, and I smiled at the thought of Mama dangling her feet over the bank of a river in Paradise. I believe that's when she heard the words of our Lord. "Well done, good and faithful servant," as He wrapped His arms around her and led her home.

Be joyful always; pray continually.

(I Thessalonians 5:16-17)

—Sue Tornai

Prayer Nugget

The traditional family unit is God's idea, designed and created as a place for God to fulfill His plan through—a plan for relationship and love and nurturing.

Heavenly Father, thank You for my family that You chose to place me in. Help me love them, honor them, and pray for them always. In Jesus' name I pray. Amen

_____

_____

_____

_____

_____

_____

_____

_____

_____

_____

_____

_____

_____

_____

_____

_____

_____

_____

Chapter 5

GIFTS THAT KEEP ON GIVING

CLOSE ENCOUNTERS

LAST NIGHT MY daughter, Molly, and I had a close encounter with a snake. I'll spare you the details. Suffice it to say he was huge and just inches from my arm when I saw him, sang opera, kicked myself in the back of the head trying to get away, then spent half an hour hyperventilating and reliving it in my mind.

For the next several months I'll imagine snakes everywhere I look. I won't set foot outside without scanning the grass, the sidewalk, the bushes, and the trees for something long and skinny and scaly. I'll check under the covers before I get in bed and even under the toilet seat.

People who aren't afraid of snakes can't understand. They can tell me the snake is harmless—"the good kind of snake to have around"—all they want. That does not compute. It's a snake, and I don't care how many rodents it kills and that it means me no harm. The mere sight of it will leave me upset for literally months. The only thing that helped me calm down last night was Molly. She was clearly more upset than I was, and it seemed the motherly thing to do was to forget myself and try to comfort her. I hugged her. She cried and shook and replayed the scene for me. As if I could forget!

We called a neighbor who, instead of killing the thing, chased it right into my flowerbed and told me what a good snake it is to have there. Thanks for nothing.

An hour later, Molly and I were driving to meet my husband and son at the ballpark. I was calculating how close we'd have to walk to the overgrown backfield that looks like snake paradise when Molly asked, "Mom, how can I stop feeling so scared?"

"Let's ask God to help us." We talked a bit about how God made snakes, and just because we can't appreciate their beauty and usefulness doesn't take away from the fact that they're His creation, just like we are. Then it happened. You know how God tells us to hide His Word in our hearts and that the Holy Spirit will recall it to our mind when we need it? Well, it happened!

As we were talking, I remembered what it says about fear in 2 Timothy 1:7, "God has not given us a spirit of fear but of power and of love and self-discipline." We talked about the fact that if God didn't give us the fear we were feeling, it must come from the enemy, and do we want anything that came from him? Then I remembered that I can do all things through God, because he strengthens me.

I asked Molly if she really believed that. In my heart I was asking myself the same question. *This is just how it's supposed to work,* I thought. God's promises were rising to the top of my mind, and I was ready to claim them. Just as Christ did when the devil tempted Him in the desert, I was pulling out my weapon—the Word of God—ready to say, "It is written . . ." Molly and I were ready to pray now. We repeated those promises and told God we wanted to stand on them. We asked Him in Jesus' name to take away our fear. Next thing we knew, we were caught up in a little league game and the snake was forgotten.

That is until this morning. When Molly and I saw the snake, we were looking into my flowerbed where I'd carefully arranged all the plants I was going to plant today. I'd spent a long time at the nursery selecting them, given great thought to where each one would grow best, and had allotted time this morning to get them in the ground. After I dropped the kids off at school, I stood staring at those plants, the bags of top soil and mulch, the special time-release plant food, my gardening tools, even my CD player so I could listen to worship music while I played in the dirt. I love gardening!

Now I stood there frozen, knowing good and well I wasn't going anywhere near that flowerbed where a snake had been just fourteen hours before. Where was he now? Those plants could die in their pots for all I cared. It didn't matter that our neighbor had assured me he was harmless. "A little, old chicken snake. Just chase him away with the garden hose if he bothers you."

I didn't care how many times my husband reminded me, "He's more afraid of you than you are of him." Impossible! Then I thought of Molly. I pictured her coming home from school, seeing the plants still in their pots and knowing I'd been too scared to plant them. She wouldn't say a word, but what would register in her little mind? That I was still scared in spite of the prayer we'd said last night. What would that say to her about the power of prayer—about the ability and desire of God to help us? About her mother's faith?

I remembered the promises God had recalled to my mind. *Oh, come on, Lord,* I thought. *Can't You just send someone else to do the planting and let Molly assume it was me?* I walked over to my porch rocker and sat down—after checking underneath for you-know-who. I sat and tried to get alone with God. I remembered how my heart had gone out to Molly last night when she was so scared, and sitting there it occurred to me that my heavenly Father cared as much—even more—about how I was feeling right now. After all, He was the one who'd sent those verses to comfort me.

Do you know what I did next? I pulled on my gardening gloves and planted those plants. It was a little tense at first, but by the sixth or seventh one I was singing. I knew I wasn't alone. I looked at the cards that came with each plant—the ones with planting instructions and that best-case-scenario picture. If I do everything exactly right—give it the perfect soil, the right amount of water, the exact amount of sun—it might actually look like this one day.

I wondered if God has a best-case-scenario picture for me. With the Word of God to feed me and just the right amount of Son, what could I turn out to be? I dug my holes, added my topsoil, and got everything just where I wanted it. I fed and mulched, watered and weeded. By the time I picked Molly up from school, my garden looked spectacular. We stood there together, admiring my efforts, and imagined how it would all look in a year or two.

"But, Mom, weren't you scared?" she asked. "What about the snake?"

"I won't lie to you, Mol," I said. "I was plenty scared at first. Then I remembered that I'm a child of the Most High King, and princesses aren't afraid." She laughed. "I tried to remember some of my favorite verses like 2 Corinthians 12:9." We recited it together: "My grace is sufficient for you, for my strength is made perfect in weakness."

And Proverbs 18:10. I let Molly take that one: "The name of the LORD is a tall tower; the righteous run to it and are safe."

"The weirdest thing happened when I was planting with my face up close to the porch. I felt a cool—almost cold—breeze coming from under the house and realized why that snake was there in the first place. That old fellow was just looking for a place to get out of the heat. You know, when I realized that, for about a nanosecond I actually felt tenderness toward him."

"You're weird, Mom."

"I know." I laughed. "But I ain't afraid of no snakes." Well, not right now anyway.

—*Mimi Greenwood Knight*

AND THERE WAS MUSIC IN THE AIR

Spicy breezes tossed the wet baby clothes as I hung them on the roof of our apartment-hotel in Tegucigalpa, Honduras. We were there to adopt our infant daughter, Kika, along with her sister, Maria. I enjoyed doing laundry, looking out over red roofs at the green bowl of the encircling mountains. Often as I worked, I heard music in the air. Somewhere nearby an orchestra was playing. The beautiful sounds lifted my tired spirit.

As the girls grew, they joined their older brother at our small Christian school. The boys in Kika's class teased her mercilessly, and she felt stupid—as if she had come away empty-handed when talents were handed out. I prayed she would find her special gift.

Kika didn't study music as a child beyond a couple years of very basic piano. In fourth grade, while public school kids were trying different instruments and starting lessons, her school had no band program. Even the piano lessons came to a stop when her teacher moved away, and her successor bluntly told Kika she just wasn't very musical. Needless to say, this crushed her.

In seventh grade, she started attending the public middle school. A couple of weeks into September, she called from school—apparently not able to wait till she came home that night—and told me, "I think I want to start playing clarinet in the band."

I was startled, to say the least. "Um, sure. What do we have to do?"

She asked me to call the band director. When I did, he said, "She will need to take private lessons for a full year first. If she does that, I'll put her in with the third clarinets when she's in eighth grade. It's not going to be easy," he warned me. "These other kids have been playing for three years already. She has an awful lot of catching up to do."

Kika scarcely heard the warnings. She was just so thrilled to be getting a chance to play. We lined up a teacher and rented an instrument, which Kika immediately began trying to assemble in the car on the way home. That Sunday, before she'd even had her first lesson, the church music director posted a sign-up sheet for musicians to volunteer to play for the Christmas service. Kika immediately added her name, and in parentheses, "clarinet."

We loved Kika's new teacher from the first moment, but she also told her she'd have a hard road. She was impressed, though, when Kika told her she needed to be able to play for Christmas. "What an attitude!" Kika practiced every day.

I loved waking up Saturday mornings and hearing her basic notes already rising from the screened porch, greeting the dawn. Before she first picked up the clarinet, she had been self-conscious and undirected. Now, her love for music and her new sense of competence seemed like the spring rains, bringing surging new growth. Her teacher, amazed at her progress, said, "I've had some wonderful students, but nobody like her. She's incredibly motivated."

As a Christian, she also saw something else. "You have a gift from God," she told her, "and along with that gift comes responsibility."

Advent arrived. Christmas morning, as worshippers arrived for church, Kika greeted them with a selection of three simple carols. I held my breath, but she made it through with hardly a squeak.

The next summer, her teacher took a vacation from teaching all her students except for Kika, who played and played and played. Another fall came, and she joined the band as promised. She had scarcely started when she set a new goal. "I want to play bassoon," she announced, and within a few weeks of starting lessons on the school's ancient and battered instrument, she became the middle school band's entire bassoon section.

"She's a real asset," the band director told me. He couldn't believe she hadn't touched any instrument at all before the previous fall. In tenth grade, she auditioned into honors band and on up through regional band and orchestra, then wept bitterly when the all-state band eluded her. She felt as if her fairytale ascent had ended.

We tried to tell her she'd had an amazing year for a sophomore—especially one who had started playing so late. But her soaring spirits crashed, along with her sense of having found her calling. All through that year of auditions she had prayed for success—to do well and find favor. She had often marveled at the miracle of God's bringing her from third-world poverty to a place where playing the bassoon was even possible. It had seemed like destiny, but now she wasn't so sure.

That summer, when Kika and Maria turned sixteen, and their older brother, Tony, also adopted from Honduras, turned eighteen, we took a family vacation to Tegucigalpa, leaving behind the music and the pain it represented for a while. We went back to explore their roots. The wonderful smells and colors and sounds will remain with us forever.

We returned to the same hotel where all three children had come as infants and we had first become a family. The hotel owner remembered us on sight and greeted us like long-lost relatives. I could scarcely wait till the next day's light when I could show the kids the view from the rooftop.

The next morning I climbed the steps and came out into the fragrant rooftop breezes I remembered so well. For a moment, my mind drifted back over the years to the weariness of being a young mother carrying heavy baskets of wet laundry up those same steps and the sense of peace this beautiful place had brought me. Then, suddenly, I heard the music.

"Kika!" I rushed to call her to the roof. "Hurry!"

As she burst out of the shadowy stairwell into the sunlight, she immediately saw what I had never really noticed: across a side street from the hotel was the National Conservatory of Music! While we looked down in amazement, the orchestra took a rehearsal break. The doors along the second floor portico opened, and a young musician came out, carrying a bassoon.

In that moment, the sun on our heads felt like God's hand of blessing. As a newborn, Kika had come here to begin her journey toward her destiny, accompanied by the sound of classical music, so rare in the Tegucigalpa streets. And now, when that destiny seemed to be slipping away, God had brought her back where she had begun to reaffirm His plan for her life.

The Lord will fulfill his purpose for me.

(Psalm 138:8)

—Susan Kimmel Wright

TWINS AND TALENT

All my life, God has always been *right there*. When I called out to Him, He was there. I have always known He would answer my prayers, because that is just what He does.

One of my earliest memories of answered prayer occurred when my twin brother and I were in a talent show in grade school. But it wasn't just a grade school talent show. At the time, we lived in a small, rural community in Oklahoma, and the talent show included the high school, junior high, and grade school.

Randy and I had sung together from my earliest memories. Our daddy was a minister and evangelist. From the time we could stand and sing, we stood on chairs behind the pulpit before he ministered and sang for the glory of the Lord. Singing in front of people was not new to me, and even in the fifth grade, I wanted to do my very best because I knew the Lord's presence was everywhere. I wanted to do my best for Him.

I remember praying, *Lord, even if we don't win, please allow us to do well in the contest.*

Two contestants from each grade level were entered. This seemed like an unfair advantage, because it meant younger students competed with seniors in high school.

My mother spent a lot of time practicing with us to make sure every note was right in tune. When the big day arrived, we had chosen two songs to sing. The first was a cutie song, "Let Me Kiss You." The crowd showed its pleasure when we ended the song with me kissing my brother on the cheek. "Oh, how cute!" and similar comments echoed across the auditorium.

Our second song, "Believe, You Must Believe," was our statement of faith. Even in fifth grade we were singing songs of faith and what we believed.

After everyone had performed, the judges were tasked with selecting a winner. My twin brother and I waited backstage with the other contestants. We all waited with bated breath in anticipation of the announcement—even the older, more experience contestants.

Finally, the big moment came. Second and third-place winners were named first, but our names were not called. My heart skipped a beat. Could it be? Would we be the school talent show champions—or nothing at all?

Then from the podium we heard, "And this year's talent show champions are Kandy and Randy Sharp!" I knew deep in my heart that it wasn't our amazing talent but an answer to a simple, childlike prayer of faith.

> I will say of the Lord, "He is my refuge and my fortress, my God, in whom I trust."
>
> (Psalm 91:2)

*—**Kandy Sharp***

SAFE AND DRY

Easter was fast approaching, and I was out shopping for my children's outfits. My son was one, and my daughter was four. We had been to two stores, and Kellee's outfit was complete: a frilly slip to go with the Daisy Kingdom dress I'd made for her, white stockings, and black patent leather shoes. But I still needed socks for Billy.

He had a simple little suit but hated wearing shoes, so I'd opted for just socks. The last store I went to had good prices on some household items I needed, and I found the socks. The end of a long afternoon was in sight as I waited at the checkout line.

An unwelcome chill in the air greeted us when we left the store, and I was beginning to feel hungry. I loaded the kids and bag into the car and reached for my purse. Then I noticed the socks sitting in the bottom of the cart below, but not directly under, my purse. "Oh, no! The socks!" I exclaimed as I reached into my pocket to check the receipt.

"What's wrong?" my daughter asked.

"I didn't pay for the socks," I said as I finished reading the receipt. I wondered if I should take them anyway and come back the next day to pay for them. But I wasn't sure Kellee would understand that. She might think I was stealing, and I didn't want her to have a negative image of me for even a day.

Putting my purse and kids back in the cart, we trudged into the store. Customer service had a long line, so I went to my cashier and explained the situation. She had just closed up but thanked me for my honesty and let me pay for the socks.

By now it was a little cooler outside, and we were definitely hungry. When we returned home, I pulled into the garage and opened the back door for the kids. As I unbuckled my son's car seat, I noticed my purse was missing. A thorough search of the car came up empty. It wasn't there.

I buckled a fussy little boy back in and told Kellee to buckle back up. And we drove back to the store.

Oh, Lord, please let my purse be safe at the checkout stand, I prayed aloud. I couldn't imagine it staying safe if I'd left it in the cart in the parking lot. That day God answered part of my prayer. He kept my purse safe—in the parking lot! We had been parked on the outskirts of the lot, where it would have been easy to reach into the cart, grab the purse, and keep walking.

We didn't even park. I just pulled right up to the cart, jumped out of the car, and grabbed my purse. Holding it up, I said, "Kellee, look! Isn't God great?"

I was so excited to show my daughter that God answers prayer, even when I do dumb things like leave my purse unattended in a cart near a lamppost where would-be thieves lurk.

For the eyes of the Lord move to and fro throughout the earth, to shew himself strong in the behalf of them whose heart is perfect towards him.

(II Chronicles 16:9a KJV)

—*Lisa Keck*

God-Incidence

"Mommy, I saw that angel by my bed again," announced my four-year-old daughter, Christina, as she joined her brothers for breakfast.

Again? I wasn't even aware of a previous time. I resisted the urge to call our pediatrician and remained calm. "What did the angel say, Honey?" Secretly, I hoped the so-called angel had a verbal message.

"Nothing. She just always smiles at me. And sometimes Barbara is with her." I swallowed hard. Barbara was my niece who had passed away nearly two years before my Christina was born.

Coincidence? Or God-incidence?

I thought it odd that this incident occurred on the very day my daughter had an appointment with a specialist to determine why she had developed five, dime-to-nickel-sized cysts on her hands, knees, and ankles. I feared the worst—a childhood cancer diagnosis. And Christina's angel visitation didn't do anything to relieve my anxiety.

When I confided Christina's experience to my close friend, Kathy, she felt that the angel-and-Barbara encounter was an assurance of a positive outcome. "Even though you didn't see the angel, I think your daughter's experience is a sign to you. I think maybe God is telling you that He is taking care of your little girl, and you have no need to worry. Christina is in His capable hands."

It turned out she was right. My daughter was diagnosed with juvenile rheumatoid arthritis (JRA). I breathed a deep breath of relief and prayed. *Thank You, Lord. With Your help, I know I can handle junior RA better than cancer.* We were referred to a JRA clinic but had to wait five weeks before Christina could be examined and treated.

In the meantime, our pediatrician advised us to see an ophthalmologist to check for evidence of JRA in Christina's eyes. I explained to my daughter that she would be seeing an eye doctor, and she became very excited. "Oh, good! I can't wait to see my friend, Hope. She told me she goes to the eye doctor too. That's where she gets her glasses."

I explained that Hope probably doesn't go to the same doctor, so it was unlikely we would see her there. But Christina was sure she would. *Oh well, at least she's not afraid to go.*

"Hope! Hope! Hope! Mommy, I told you Hope would be here."

While the girls hugged, I silently prayed. *Father, I'm hoping for the very best diagnosis and outcome for Christina today. And Hope is here.* Peace and optimism replaced my fear and anxiety.

Coincidence? Or God-incidence?

"Does everything look fuzzy to you?" Hope reached for my daughter. And Christina did the same. Both of the girls had just had their eyes dilated, and while they waited to be reexamined, they danced about the room, finally falling into a giggling heap.

I thought about Hope's question regarding fuzzy vision. So much was still fuzzy with regard to Christina's health. And finances were tight as my husband's company was in the middle of reorganization, which included significant salary reductions. *God, You know all things. You know the desires and dreams I have for my little girl.*

I envisioned Christina in a room featuring her loud, favorite colors: fuchsia and orange. In the corner of her room stood a tiny replica of my own dream kitchen. A room fit for a princess. But how would we afford such luxuries for our little girl? And would she enjoy them if we could?

Each night, after Christina fell fast asleep, I tiptoed into her small room, not the room I dreamed of for her, but the tiny room just off the hall from the room my husband and I shared. She looked like a tiny angel resting under her comforter. I wondered if her angel was looking in on her too.

Each night—unbeknown to our little princess—I checked her body for any possible new lumps. One night, I felt so alone and heavy with the weight of worry that I wondered if anyone really cared. Did anyone care about our daughter and what she was facing in her young life? Did God care? I wondered if anyone noticed that my desires for Christina were only a dream away. They might as well have been thousands of miles beyond my reach.

A few days later, I attended a ladies Bible study for moms. I had been a regular part of this group for some time but hadn't shared my tiny "kitchen wish" with anyone there. Yet, a friend of mine came over and asked, "Would you like a kitchen set? You know, a play-set for Christina to play with?" I couldn't believe what she was asking me.

Coincidence? Or God-incidence?

She wrote out the directions to another friend's house. "Lisa's little girl has outgrown the little kitchenette, and she asked if I might know someone who would want it. You and Christina came to mind."

The next morning I drove to Lisa's house. Besides the play kitchen, Lisa had set aside a gently used hot-pink and orange comforter. I gazed closer at the design. Disney princesses peered back at me. I was certain a bargain angel had been listening to me late the other night.

Again, coincidence or God-incidence?

As soon as I got home, I called my sister, Kathy, and poured out my grateful heart to her. My big sister told me that everything I was experiencing was God's way of listening to my heart, even when I wasn't formally praying, and that He was with me when I felt alone in my worry for Christina.

JRA Clinic Day at Children's Hospital arrived, and fortunately, we lived close by. I remember listening to stories of so many others who had driven for hours to our medical hub city. Hand in hand, Christina and I maneuvered around several examination stations. We spoke with nutritionists, social workers, and physical therapists. My daughter had her vitals taken and blood drawn before seeing the rheumatologist. During the multi-hour visit, we chatted with other children, some in wheelchairs and others with moderate symptoms of JRA.

A teenage girl, who appeared quite unaffected, struck up a conversation with my daughter. She explained to Christina that she had been diagnosed with JRA around the age of four. Aside from yearly check-ups with a rheumatologist, she had lived symptom-free for many years. She chatted sweetly with Christina and then asked a random question, phrased more as a statement, "You like princesses, don't you?" God, once again, was reminding me that my daughter was a princess in God's kingdom. A daughter of the King of kings.

Coincidence or God-incidence?

Minutes later it was our turn in the rheumatologist's back room, and he confirmed Christina's JRA. Thankfully, she had a mild case, and over the next two years her flares occurred only one to three times per week, erupting during sleep, much like an older person with osteoarthritis. Physical overexertion could also trigger an attack, so we monitored Christina's physical activities to make sure she stayed beneath the threshold of a flare. Her medication was minimal, and we joined the Arthritis Foundation to learn as much as we could about prevention.

We enrolled our daughter in year-around swimming to help her muscles and joints, and we learned what trigger foods to avoid. She attended school with all the other neighborhood children, and besides the medications—and occasional flares—continued living the active life of a normal four-year-old.

The years passed, and as Christina got older she began to question why she needed to see the doctor more often than her brothers. Until then she had not questioned her JRA. She still had intermittent symptoms but didn't understand that she was battling a condition that could have been crippling in its extreme form. My husband and I never thought to explain something we knew she couldn't understand at such a young age. We were concerned that if we tried, the explanation might define or isolate her from her peers. But the time had come.

After our conversation, Christina responded by drawing hearts on paper. "I guess I am good at art because I have arthritis." She stamped a smile on our hearts with her words. My husband and I knew at that moment that our daughter realized she had a very real condition, but it certainly did not have her.

Friends and family continued to pray that Christina would be completely healed from JRA. A few weeks later, the flares lessoned substantially and began occurring only three to four months apart. Then her arthritis symptoms became nonexistent.

"Your daughter is a very lucky girl. She's in remission." I'll never forget the day the doctor declared Christina JRA free.

Yes, a lucky girl, but even more than that, our now eight-year-old daughter is healed by the Great Physician's hand. Hope, answered prayers, and an angel—though unseen by me—offered glimpses of constant hope through uncertain circumstances.

Coincidence? No.

God-incidence? Yes, without a doubt.

Beloved, I wish above all things that thou mayest prosper and be in health, even as thy soul prospereth.

(3 John 3 KJV)

—Lisa Plowman Dolensky

Prayer Nugget

Did you know that God gives gifts? Skills, abilities, and talents unique to us are gifts from Him. Life is a gift. He is the original gift-giver. He gave us His Son, the greatest gift ever given. Ask the Lord to help you identify the gifts He's given you. List them below.

Father, I thank You for the many gifts You've blessed me with—my life, and all it holds. Most of all, I thank You for the gift of your Son, Jesus. Enable me to be a gift to others. In Jesus' name I pray. Amen.

_____

_____

_____

_____

_____

_____

_____

_____

_____

_____

_____

_____

_____

_____

_____

_____

_____

Chapter 6

YOU'LL NEVER GUESS
WHAT HAPPENED!

⤳⧼⧽◎

THE GOD WHO SEES

SWEAT TRICKLED DOWN my back as I squinted into the late-afternoon African sun. Trying to focus, I fought panic. Glances directed my way made me aware I was becoming the center of attention. *Take a deep breath. Look confident. Don't cry. Think.*

This "trip of a lifetime" had been in the planning for four years. Now, my kids and I were beginning in Kenya, traveling north through the Middle East, then wandering through Europe until we finished in Scotland many months later.

I confidently explained to skeptical friends and relatives that my goal was to teach my kids about their world and how it works. They told me I was irresponsible and crazy. In my heart, what I really wanted was to instill values, say important parental things to them, and really get to know them before they grew up and were gone. A great plan, but it crashed on the very first day.

Our near-empty flight arrived in Nairobi, Kenya, at 4 A.M. on January 2, 2008. The country was rapidly descending into ethnic violence following charges of fraud in the recent presidential elections. Nairobi itself was relatively calm, and we were meeting up with a local friend, so we initially decided to hunker down and wait it out. However, memories of Rwandan-style anarchy and sensational news footage of burning and looting prompted terrified telephone calls from loved ones begging us to evacuate. So, after some hasty middle-of-the-night arrangements, we arrived in Dar es Salaam, Tanzania, with no destination, no plans, and no contacts.

We caught the attention of immigration officials right from the start—a woman traveling alone with two children. A large, angry official began questioning us almost immediately: "Where is the children's father? Why are you here? What is your itinerary?" What answers I could give were clearly unsatisfactory. When he allowed us to continue to Immigration and present our visa applications, his rage finally exploded when he discovered our biggest problem: we did not have enough cash to pay for the visas. I begged and pleaded in response to his threats and was finally allowed to exit the airport to search for an ATM to withdraw the money I needed. My children, however, would be held until my return. I could see the fear in their eyes, and I'm sure they could see the tears forming in mine as I assured them I would be gone only a few minutes to get the money, and that it would be all right.

But I couldn't, and it wasn't. For a variety of reasons, I was locked out of all my bank accounts. I stood there in the sticky tropical heat, friendless and very far from home, fighting panic and struggling to carefully think through my resources one more time, looking for one I had missed. I have rarely felt so alone in my life.

"Do you need some help?" The voice interrupted my thoughts, and I looked up. One of the men watching me had approached. *I must look like an easy target.* Stories of scam artists and even worse filled my thoughts.

"No, thank you. I'm just using the ATM." I struggled to inject confidence that I didn't have into my voice.

"I've been watching you, and you've tried several times now. Are you sure you're okay?" *Oh, great. He knows I'm in trouble. What should I do? If I tell him, maybe he can help me come up with an idea. Worst case, he'll know I don't have any money and target someone else. I hope.*

"I need three hundred U.S. dollars to pay for visas." There, it was out. Tears threatened again, but I fought them back.

Calmly, he reached into his pocket and pulled out a neatly folded bundle of bills, peeled off three brand new one-hundred-dollar bills, and handed them to me.

I was shocked. *Should I take it? Will it cost me something I don't want to pay?* With no other options, I decided to accept it. "Thank you," I managed to stammer out. "I can pay you back as soon as I can get to a bank." He handed me a business card. "I'm sure they are also asking you for contact information inside. Use my information. You can send me the money when you have it." How did he know? And with that, he walked away.

I reentered the immigration hall, paid the fees, endured more hassle from the irritated officials, collected my children, and proceeded to customs to find our luggage, which, of course, was torn apart and scattered everywhere.

As we gathered our belongings, a young woman approached us. She introduced herself and explained that the man who had given us the money was her father. As I began to profusely express my thanks, she told us that he was still concerned about us, and knowing I was reluctant to talk to a strange man, he sent her in to offer us further help, possibly a ride to a hotel?

I thought about this. We had no money for a cab; I didn't know how far it was into the city or even if I could use my credit card on my now-frozen accounts. On the other hand, what did I know about this man? His business card said he had a job with a large oil company, which probably meant he wasn't a scam artist. I recognized the young woman as a fellow passenger on my flight, so I knew his story about waiting for his family was probably legitimate. It might be safer to actually trust this stranger than to face the city alone. I hoped. I was exhausted, and I accepted the ride. I also accepted his invitation for a hot meal, prepared by his wife, and badly needed rest in their spare bedroom.

Hours later I awoke with a clearer head and more stable emotions and went out to meet our hosts. Albert and Esther were two of the most hospitable people I've ever met, and I enjoyed getting to know them. As I told them our story of how we came to be in the Tanzania airport in such a helpless state, Albert listened sympathetically. When I finished my story, he smiled and proceeded to tell his own story of how he had resisted the clear direction of God to approach a strange woman in an airport and repeatedly offer help in spite of her rejection. I smiled ruefully and remembered that I had rejected his offer for help no less than three times before he finally sent his daughter instead. He reached into his back pocket and pulled out a worn copy of Oswald Chambers' *My Utmost for His Highest* and wanted to show me the entry for January 2, the day we had arrived in Nairobi. He said the message was for me. It was entitled, "Will You Go Without Knowing?"

As he read the text aloud, I realized in my soul that although I had been very far from home and help, and no one knew of my desperation, my God did. He is the God who sees, and He saw me. Not only did He see me, He also sent one of His own to provide what I needed, both physically and spiritually. I don't need to be afraid.

Tears I had fought so long finally flowed.

The Lord is my shepherd, I shall not want.

(Psalm 23:1 KJV)

—Denise Chang

A DIVINE APPOINTMENT

God arranges divine appointments of which we are unaware. Such was the case on this dark night. Due to severe weather moving in, we canceled our weekly prayer meeting. In the event someone unexpected might arrive, I drove to the church, turned on the lights, and waited.

Sure enough, a dark pick-up truck that I didn't recognize drove in and parked near the door. With some trepidation, I walked outside to greet whoever was driving. Down went the window, and I recognized a Christian woman I had not seen in quite some time.

"Helen, what are you doing out on such a stormy night?"

"Well, I came to the prayer meeting."

Having driven a long way, she proceeded to get out. Then I noticed the oxygen cannulae in her nostrils and a canister strapped to her side.

"We cancelled the meeting because of the weather, but come on in."

Once inside the church, we moved down the aisle to the front row where, as always, I was aware of the large backlit cross and its import above the platform before us. Helen and I had known each other a long time, and I was surprised to see her on oxygen. She had always been strong, sturdy, and was a Bible teacher herself.

"Whatever are you doing on oxygen?"

"I had a near-death experience in reaction to medication and a wild ambulance ride to the emergency room."

The E.R. doctor told her she was lucky to have made it and that most people with such a reaction die en route. She had suffered a sudden, severe reaction to several antibiotics for a lung condition. She was placed in the intensive care unit for the next two weeks, and she was told she would be on oxygen for the rest of her life and must avoid future use of antibiotics.

"On top of all this, my son is in federal prison for running drugs out of South America with his own airplane."

But having great faith in God, and having seen miracles of deliverance through her life and mine, she smiled. "But with God's help, we'll make it!"

I realized she had come for prayer for her son, whom she had reared in the faith, and for her physical condition that she had been told was irreversible. As we sat there, we began to discuss days when we had seen

God move wondrously in meetings. As we recalled various occasions with startling answers to prayer, we became lifted up in our spirits and were having a wonderful time. Soon, we both became intensely aware of the presence of the Lord with us. Then, slowly but surely, we experienced a great power showering down upon us. We were hushed in awe, our faces upturned, our hearts burning with the love of God as tears of adoration flowed at such a visitation from on high. Neither of us spoke; we asked nothing of Him. It was a holy moment of deepest worship. After a time, the presence of the Lord slowly lifted. We turned and stared at each other in amazement.

Then slowly—deliberately—she removed the oxygen from her nose and turned it off. Faces beaming, we both knew she was healed. We arose, embraced, and rejoiced, thanking and praising God. We said our good-byes, and she went on her way.

Three years later, at a chance meeting in a nearby eatery, I saw her again. She was looking great, and her son, who had received an early release from prison, was also doing well. All glory be to God!

> And a book of remembrance was written before him for them that feared the LORD, and that thought upon his name. And they shall be mine saith the Lord of hosts, in that day when I make up my jewels; and I will spare them, as a man spareth his own son that serveth him."
> (Malachi 3:16-17 KJV)

—Twilah A. Fox, M.D.

THE PERFECT STORM—OUR PERFECT GOD

Hurricane Ike had taken its toll on the Houston area. For seven straight days we were without electricity, running water, and fast food. And to top it all off—school was cancelled indefinitely!

We knew our prayers were answered when there was no damage to our home from falling trees. Hurricane force winds, however, had coaxed every loose branch from the heavily laden tree boughs on our two-acre property. We were, literally, left to pick up the pieces.

Two straight days of hauling limbs, branches, and leaves resulted in three debris piles more than eight feet high each. Much to my chagrin, the wet rubbish mountains refused to burn—even after a shot of fuel.

What do you do when you can't bathe or check your e-mail, and you don't want to go in the house to three grumpy kids and a husband who smell worse than you do? You sit in your lawn chair, stare at the rubbish pile that won't burn, and try to count your blessings.

Gazing at the fire that wasn't, I remembered how the day following the storm a strong cold front blew through southeast Texas. As a resident for forty-plus years, I knew how rare that was. Temperatures usually drift into the nineties until much later in the year. Instead, gorgeous crisp days were followed by nippy sweater-weather nights. Air conditioning? Who needs it! My God is gracious.

I also thought about the majestic oaks, pines, and sweet-gum trees surrounding our country home. God, in His goodness, held them in place. I know that many didn't fare nearly as well as we did, and my prayers were with them. *Please, dear ones, remember: this is a season, and good or bad, every season eventually comes to an end.* My God is merciful.

Another blessing I realized was the benefit of a vacation from television. My two sons and daughter probably didn't see it for the blessing it was. We didn't do the generator thing like so many affected by the hurricane. If it didn't run on batteries, we didn't use it. Instead, we used our imaginations. We played cards. We found a stash of glow sticks and had a lights out party. We talked, we fought, and I listened and found out important prayer needs in my kids' lives. It's hard to talk, listen, or use your imagination with the television on. So, He took it away. My God is resourceful.

I also used the time for intense prayer and communion with my heavenly Father. My world slowed down. I can't remember the last time I sat in the yard, patiently waiting for a pile of soggy limbs and brush to burn. But as I sat there, I spoke to God. I thanked Him for His blessings, and I listened to Him speak to my heart. I pointed to a gangly, dead oak tree hovering above the rubbish pile, completely unscathed by the hurricane-force winds, and prayed, *Lord, the only thing that would have made Ike the perfect storm is if that dead tree would have blown over into the brush pile so I could burn it when things dry out.*

That's when it happened.

I noticed fire falling from the sky. My two teenagers later teased that it was raining fire and brimstone. Looking up, I noticed the forty-foot-tall crest of the dead oak tree was aflame. How could it have happened? My fizzled flame wouldn't toast a marshmallow. Then, the falling embers floated over and ignited my stubborn brush pile! At that moment, I realized the magnificence of the almighty God I serve.

The oak tree continued burning for fifteen days. Little by little, pieces were consumed by fire and dropped into the burn pile that I couldn't even persuade to ignite. People who have seen or heard about the burning tree have likened it to biblical stories. One said it was like Moses' burning bush. Someone said it reminded them of the pillar of cloud by day and the pillar of fire by night because of the smoke emitted during the day and the glow bright enough to see by at night.

But I'm reminded of Elijah's fight with the prophets of Baal. You see, just like those prophets, I tried everything in my own power to get that burn pile to ignite. But the Lord in His grace provided the fire to remind me how very much He cares for and listens to His children.

I'll never forget Hurricane Ike. It was a time to cast off some things I didn't need and cling to the things that really matter. But most of all, God showed me in His own way that no matter how great I may think my idea is, His plan is always—perfect.

[Elijah said] "Then you call on the name of your god, and I will call on the name of the LORD. The god who answers by fire—He is God."

(1 Kings 18:24)

—*Annette O'Hare*

Shanghai Encounter

The most dramatic and astonishing answer to prayer I ever experienced involved a Chinese boy named Eric.

As my husband, George, and I stood on a street corner in Shanghai, pondering over a map of the city, a young man approached us. "May I help you?" he asked in English. His name was Eric, and he was eager to improve his English. Since he had the afternoon free, he offered to accompany us on our walking tour.

Eric was a very friendly young man, the same age as our son. He had an inquiring mind and a sensitive nature. In spite of our language differences, he was easy to relate to. He and my husband soon found a common interest in classical music and American sports. Praying for an opening to talk about my Christian faith and ask about his beliefs, I threw up a trial balloon during a break in the conversation.

"Do you practice Buddhism?" I asked.

"No," he said, "religion is just for old people. The young people in China don't have a religion."

We went into a department store, looking for a specific souvenir. Dreamy, poignant, wistful music floated through the open atrium as we ascended many levels on the escalator. "What is that music?" I asked.

"'I Wish for You,'" he replied. Immediately I sensed an open door for the conversation I wanted to initiate.

"In your country, what should I wish for a young man of your age?"

"A nice home," he responded. Earlier he had revealed that he was an only child and lived with his devoted parents in the countryside outside the city.

"In our beliefs," I commented, "we have a wonderful home prepared and awaiting us in our eternal life in heaven." We stepped off the escalator at a food court for a soft drink and snack. As we searched for an isolated table, I silently asked God to give me an opportunity to share with Eric the love and the hope we've found in our Christian faith.

I posed the question, "Did you ever hear the story of the first man and woman?"

"Adam and Sara," he said, beaming, pleased that he knew the names.

"Adam and Eve," I gently corrected, and began telling him the story of the perfect garden home provided for them by their Creator. As I spoke of their choice to disobey God that resulted in sin, I discovered Eric had no concept of sin. It was a challenge to talk to a person who had no preconceived ideas or spiritual teaching. His spirit was completely blank. I had to rely on the Holy Spirit to guide my words and impart truth to Eric.

I began to tell Eric how much God loved him. We had learned that he had a very loving relationship with his parents. I suggested that if he could multiply their love for him a zillion times, that would give him some concept of how much God loved him.

A word picture came to my mind, and I asked, "When you call your father in the country, do you ever get a busy signal or does he refuse to answer? If you accept God as your father, you never get a busy signal, he is always home. We call that prayer."

His face brightened as he said, "You mean I could pray anytime?"

My husband was supporting with silent prayer and occasional comments. He told me later that Eric reminded him of the rabbits we often see in our backyard at home in Kentucky. They sit up on their hind legs, and their ears are perked up at full attention. Eric appeared to be totally absorbed with the idea of God as his father.

I told him the steps he would follow if he decided he wanted to ask God to be his father, which included confessing Jesus Christ as his Lord and Savior. My husband told Eric we would like to bless him with some Christian printed materials or a Bible, but we didn't know if receiving these by mail would put him in jeopardy. Eric told us his girlfriend's grandmother was a Christian and said he wanted to buy a Bible.

We resumed our meandering with Eric on the streets of Shanghai. It started to rain, so we took a taxi back to the hotel. Eric went with us, since his bus route to the countryside was in the same direction. As I sat with him in the back seat, I told him, "You have been so kind to us, spending the afternoon directing and helping us."

"And you told me about God and Jesus!" he replied with enthusiasm.

As we left the taxi to go our separate ways, I gave him a hug and said, "I hope we meet again."

"We will meet again," Eric responded in a dreamy tone.

For the next couple of days Eric's eternal destiny continued to consume my thoughts. I could not forget his shining face when I told him about the heavenly Father. I constantly prayed for him while completing our tour schedule. Finally, I was able to release him to the Lord.

George and I returned to the U.S. with an overnight stay in Portland, Oregon. While George napped in our room, I sat reading in the hotel lobby. A pleasant gentleman sat down on the sofa opposite me and asked what I was reading. I told him and explained that we had just returned from a trip to China.

"Have you ever been to China?" I asked.

"Several times," he replied.

I launched into the story of our encounter with Eric. He introduced himself as Dr. Dyer and said he was involved in a mission outreach that was having a board meeting in Portland. He was in the lobby to greet the people as they arrived and direct them to the meeting room.

As unbelievable as it sounds, Dr. Dyer knew a missionary couple in Shanghai. He offered to send them Eric's name for follow up. I have never had a more dramatic answer to prayer! What are the chances that a man would be in the lobby of a hotel in Portland at the exact time as a Kentucky woman burdened for the salvation of a young man in China? The odds on this same man knowing a missionary couple who later willingly agreed to contact Eric are infinitesimal.

We had one letter from Eric in response to the note and classical CDs we sent as a Christmas gift. My husband pointed out to me how difficult it would be for Eric to write in English. We wrote to Eric one more time but never heard from him again. He changed jobs, and a subsequent letter returned with no forwarding address.

We did hear from Dr. Dyer that the missionaries had contacted Eric. He was interested in becoming a Christian and said he remembered George and Peggy but had lost their address. Our encounter with Eric in Shanghai and with Dr. Dryer in Portland demonstrates what a detailed God we serve and the extent He will go to for one lost sheep.

God burdened me for Eric and provided an answer to my earnest prayer for him. The results rest with Him. I do believe Eric's parting words, "We will meet again."

The eyes of the Lord are on the righteous and his ears are attentive to their cry.

(Psalm 34:15)

—Peggy Park

ANGELS IN OVERALLS

I jerked my head toward the light trailing in our wake. A shower of sparks lit up Highway 72 like the 4th of July. "Uh oh," I murmured.

My husband cast a dark glance in my direction. "What's that?"

Knots tightened in my stomach as I peered through the dusty back window of the pickup. "Looks like the launcher." What else could go wrong today? A bead of sweat slithered down my brow.

The truck bumped along the rutted, two-lane road a little farther before Bob maneuvered onto a wide spot and slammed on the brakes. He shot another glare at me before opening his door and climbing out. He was right, of course. This was entirely my fault. My "short cut" had taken us miles from civilization into rural Mississippi.

I eased out the passenger door. Summer air hovered thick and heavy without a hint of a breeze. Insects of unnatural size buzzed past my ears. The odor of burning metal punctuated the atmosphere. I expected to find the trailer carrying our remote-control plane launcher had merely jiggled off its hitch. Instead, broken pieces dragged the pavement with only a chain connecting them to the truck. Hence, the sparks.

With a sigh, I pushed bangs off my damp forehead. Hard to gauge Bob's level of fatigue from his expression, I inched to the side opposite him so I wouldn't be too close in case he exploded.

The launcher tipped up like a stinkbug. First glance assured me it was no easy fix. We needed a welder. But where could we find one around here? Bob stretched. Back must be hurting again. And no wonder. We had driven all afternoon from Alabama on the way home to California. Memphis must be hours away. At seven o'clock on a Friday night, our hope of finding an open welding shop nearby evaporated with the stifling air.

Just ahead, a dilapidated shack crouched beside the road, isolated from electric lines. In fact, the usual line of poles that should have paralleled this highway seemed to be missing altogether. Probably no phone, either.

I pointed. Bob shrugged. We were out of choices. I painted on a faint smile. "Worth a try." I started toward the house—hope leaking away with each step.

As I approached, a stooped, gray woman emerged. She wasn't smiling. Shadows on her cheeks looked like scoops of flesh had been removed. She must be lacking teeth to hold her cheeks out. Maybe that's why she didn't smile. I gulped, trying to muster a drop of hope.

Shoulders back, friendly smile plastered in place, I walked toward her. With her head tilted to one side, she listened as I explained our woeful predicament. Her expression never changed. I paused, waiting for her answer. A river of sweat trickled down my back. I swiped my forehead, gathering moisture, and glanced at Bob for support. With his back turned, arms akimbo, he studied the launcher. No support there.

Just when I'd decided the woman didn't intend to answer, she let out a heavy sigh. "Might be a welder in Ashland," she muttered in a drawl thicker than the air. "Ain't never had no need of one. Don't know for shore."

"How far is it to Ashland?"

She flung a point in the direction we'd been headed. "Ain't far. Follow the road."

Bob unhitched the launcher, and we jumped in the truck. I watched the launcher disappear from view as we drove away. "Think it's safe to leave it there?" Bob's eyes never left the road. Expression grim, he gripped the steering wheel with clenched hands. I braced myself for the coming tirade. *Oh, Lord,* I said aloud, *please help us. We need a welder. And fast.*

As I continued to pray in silence, I studied the map from every angle, but didn't find Ashland anywhere. As far as I could tell, we were thirty or forty miles from a town in any direction, maybe more. Soon twilight would be on us.

Bob's whistling startled me. What happened to the clenched fists? His hands rested easily on the steering wheel, and a look of peace had settled over his countenance. I settled back to enjoy green fields and lush trees as they whizzed by the window. After fifteen minutes of passing fertile farms and meandering creeks, Bob's frown returned. "There's no town here. Must've gotten the direction wrong."

"Maybe it's a little farther."

Instead of a town, however, we came upon a run-down convenience store. We stopped to confirm directions and were assured that Ashland was "just down the road." No one in the huddle of teens congregated outside the market recognized the word *welder* as Bob pronounced it or knew if such a person lived in Ashland.

When we climbed back in the truck, neither of us spoke or even looked at each other.

At long last, we rounded a curve, and the tiny town of Ashland, Mississippi, spread out ahead. I scooted to the edge of my seat so I could be first to spot the welding shop. Bob drove the entire four-block perimeter. Ashland was completely deserted—not so much as a single parked car. It took less than five minutes to return to our starting point.

We stared at the empty streets. Then we faced each other. Bob's eyes were wide. "Did you see anyone? Anywhere?"

"There's not even a dog on the street!"

"Guess they've already rolled up the sidewalks." Bob tilted his head back and big guffaws rolled out of him. Belly laughs.

I joined him. Amid the laughter, he shook his head. "This could only happen to us."

That set me off giggling again. "What are we going to do?"

"Guess we'll drive to Memphis, find a welder, and persuade him to come back with us."

The sobering impossibility squelched my glee. "It'll be hours until we get to Memphis. Even if we find a welder, he won't come back tonight."

"So, we'll come back tomorrow."

Incredulous, I studied his face. *Sir, what have You done with my husband?*

"And if we can't find someone who'll come with us?"

He shrugged. "Then—we'll rent another trailer and transfer the launcher onto it."

Given its weight, the two of us could never accomplish that. "But we'll be stuck here overnight and maybe for the entire weekend. What about the delivery schedule?"

While I ticked off problems, Bob returned to driving. Without warning, he slammed on his brakes. "There's a welder right there!"

I followed his line of vision but saw only a dusty pickup moving slowly from one of the farms.

In a cloud of dust, Bob braked alongside the pickup and rolled down his window. "We have a broken rig back on Highway 72. Are you a welder?"

The farmer pulled on his chin. "I have a small welder to fix my equipment. But my son has a full-size one. I'll see if I can get him to help. If not, I'll just come on down there myself. Where're you folks broke down at?"

Bob gave directions and backed out to the road. From his expression, he didn't look like a man who'd just witnessed a miracle.

I, on the other hand, could hardly keep from shouting. "Did you see that? God answered my prayer. How did you know that was a welder?"

He glanced over his sunglasses. "Don't get excited yet. We don't know whether he can help us. We don't even know if he'll come."

But half an hour later, a fully operational mobile welding rig pulled in beside the launcher. Out stepped God's angels. The thin young man and his father, both of whom had already put in a full day of work and needed their well-earned rest, set to welding instead.

The humid July twilight gave way to darkness with no let-up on the day's heat. Soon the men were sweating profusely, but neither complained. I sat on the truck runner and watched them.

Thank You, God, for southern hospitality and for these angels in overalls You sent to help us.

About an hour and a half later, they had finished welding the pieces together with extra reinforcement on the weak areas. Better than new! Bob offered them all the cash we had, which they initially refused.

On the shack's porch, the old woman watched as she rocked in her willow chair. Jagged zigzags of light flashed from enormous thunderheads—God flexing his muscles—but it didn't rain. Counting Bob's uncharacteristic peace of mind, more than one miracle unfolded on that ordinary day.

Why does it surprise me when God answers prayer? His miracles are everywhere—like the water cycle. I don't need to worry about how problems will be resolved. God hears and answers.

I can trust His plans, because God is good.

… for your Father knows what you need, before you ask Him.

(Matthew 6:8 KJV)

—*Catherine Leggitt*

MY STOLEN BIBLE

Even though I was raised in the church, something was still missing in my life. I tried to be a good person, hoping my goodness would be enough for God, and I hoped it would get me into heaven when I died. Yet, as hard as I tried, I was never sure.

One of the things I had been curious about growing up was the Bible. Even though my family went to church most Sundays, we never had a Bible of our own. Over the years, I thought about reading it for myself someday, but I never did.

Everything changed in 1981 when I started dating a coworker at my job. After we had gone out a couple of times, she asked me, "What church do you attend?" Before I could answer, she followed it with a battery of other questions like, "Who do you think God is?" and "Have you ever read the Bible?"

I did my best to answer her questions, but I struggled. I finally confessed, "I have never read the Bible and don't even own one."

She said, "We're going to change that."

With her leading the way, we headed to a local Christian bookstore, where she purchased my first Bible. I felt both enthralled and humbled at the prospect of reading God's Word for myself. Something about holding it in my hands for the first time brought about a sense of wonder and awe.

I decided right then that I wanted this Bible to be *the* Bible for the rest of my life. Later that week, she took me to a Billy Graham Crusade, and I gave my heart to the Lord at the culmination of the message.

As the years passed, I did my best to understand everything about the Bible. I read it on a regular basis, went to weekly Bible studies, memorized parts of it, and even went to Bible college. However, on a particular day back in 1992, someone broke into my car and stole it.

When the thief saw the leather covering on my Bible, I suspect he believed it was something of value and took it. Frantic, I wondered how something like this could happen. I looked everywhere, hoping the person would realize what they had taken and discard it. My efforts proved fruitless, and I resigned myself to the fact I would never see my prized Bible again.

After a couple days of feeling discouraged, I finally decided to return to the same Christian bookstore and buy a new Bible. I wanted the exact same Bible as before, something that might help soften the feeling of loss. But the bookstore no longer carried the one I had grown to cherish. Disappointed, I couldn't bring myself to buy a new one. Of course I had prayed, asking God to bring my old Bible back. Deep down inside, though, I didn't think there was much chance of that happening.

The very next day my boss came into my office, holding something in his hand about the size of a textbook with a black leather cover. "Lynch, I think this belongs to you."

My heart was pounding when he handed it to me. A quick check let me know that my prized Bible had been found. The amazing part was that he knew nothing of what had happened. I immediately asked him, "Where did you get this?"

My boss proceeded to tell me how my Bible had been found. Seems when the thief realized the Bible wasn't of value in a monetary sense, he tossed it onto the roof of a nearby classroom. It just so happened that construction workers were doing some repairs on that particular building and came across my Bible. One of the workers picked it up and found my paycheck in the front pocket of my Bible cover. Since our paychecks are sealed in window envelopes, employees' names showed in the window. The person realized the Bible belonged to someone who worked at the school, brought it to the associate principal, who, in turn, returned it to me.

One can look at this story and think that it was a fortuitous set of circumstances that ultimately helped me retrieve my beloved Bible. The day someone took it just happened to be payday. For whatever reason, I had taken my paycheck to my car on my lunch break instead of after work as I normally did. I just happened to put my paycheck in the front pocket of my Bible, which I had never done before. The thief just happened to throw the Bible on a roof where workmen just happened to be doing repairs there a few days later. The workman who came across my Bible saw my name and decided to return it to my boss. He could just as easily have kept my Bible for himself. Instead, he felt compassion for me and returned it.

Coincidence? Possibly. What I believe is that God honored my decision back in 1981 to have that be my Bible for the rest of my life and made sure it was returned to me. I am happy to say that I still have it, happily reading each page of God's Word on a regular basis, and plan to so for the rest of my life.

Ask and and it shall be given you.

(Matthew 7:7)

—Mike Lynch

FIVE BOXES OF CHRISTMAS CARDS

I bolted for the door as the last bell in Mrs. Mitchell's fifth grade class rang that November afternoon. Outside, the overcast sky and the chill in the air sent shivers up my skinny bare legs. Mother called it typical fall weather for northeastern Oklahoma. I hurried home to get a snack and pick up my cardboard carrying case with boxed Christmas cards—my first try at door-to-door sales.

I headed out with high hopes, and knocked on every door for blocks, but found no buyers. The north wind whipped cold, and my teeth chattered as it blew a gale through my coat. My chapped lips burned, and my hands froze—numb to the handles of the case. With a runny nose and nothing to wipe it on but my coat sleeve, the urge to give up and just go home mounted. My once high hopes sunk.

In the past, my twin sister, Annette, and our little brother, Stuart, would go with Grandma Hudson to Uncle Glen's pecan groves, where we picked up pecans to earn money for Christmas. That used to be enough, but this year I needed to earn way more money. Times had changed at our house.

Daddy had died in May that year. It happened on a Friday. When Annette and I walked home for lunch, we spotted his huge dump truck parked in front of our house and ran the rest of the way. Mother met us at the door. "Shush, your daddy's asleep and doesn't feel good." Daddy never got sick. We peeked into the bedroom and watched him sleep for a minute, before heading back to school. After school, we ran home and followed close on Mother's heels when she went in to check on him.

She couldn't make him wake up, "Oh, goodness," she muttered softly with a scared look in her eyes. She ran to the phone mounted on the wall in the kitchen. I watched as she dialed Dr. Daily's office. "Hello, this is Agnes Blagg… I'm afraid something's happened to my husband… Could you come out to the house?"

He came right away, dressed in a brown suit, a striped tie, and wearing a brown hat. His kind voice, full of assurance, gave us hope, but he couldn't wake up Daddy either. He told Mother a heart attack took him.

I worried about our money and could tell mother did too. I often saw her fight back tears. She wrote down everything she spent in a little black book. One day I asked her what she was writing, and she showed me how she kept a record of our expenses. Christmas would be bleak without Daddy. Oh, how we needed him!

Darkness hovered around me, and I still had all five boxes in my carrying case. I decided to try one more door. As I walked up the driveway and knocked on the door, I whispered, "Oh God, please help me sell all five boxes." The bigness of my prayer seemed almost unreasonable.

The lady of the house answered the door right away, and I showed her my wares. Interested, she knelt down to see them. After a careful look, she asked the price. As she stood, she said, "I'll take all five boxes." I could hardly believe my ears!

All of a sudden, nothing mattered—not what Mother's little black book said, the cold north wind, or that Daddy was gone. Clutching the money, I ran home to tell everyone what had happened. We had always gone to church, and I believed in God. But this was the first time I knew through and through in my heart that God heard me, saw me, and cared for me.

'Call to me and I will answer you and tell you great and unsearchable things you do not know.'

(Jeremiah 33:3)

—Jeanette Sharp

PRAYER NUGGET

God knows our every need even before we do. He is always present and hears the silent whispers of our heart. And when He surprises us by answering our silent whispers, we stand amazed. That is our God-moment. The moment the Great I Am reveals Himself to us in a personal way.

Lord please increase my faith as I wait for Your answers. In Jesus' name I pray. Amen.

_____

_____

_____

_____

_____

_____

_____

_____

_____

_____

_____

_____

_____

_____

_____

_____

_____

_____

_____

_____

_____

_____

_____

_____

_____

_____

_____

_____

_____

_____

_____

_____

_____

_____

_____

_____

_____

_____

_____

_____

_____

Chapter 7

LOVE IS PATIENT

~∰◎

THE LIST

SINGLE BF, DESPERATELY lonely, questioning God, looking for a Christian mate. That was me eighteen years ago—disappointed with the dating scene and wondering if Mark 10:8 applied to my future at all. "And the two will become one flesh. So they are no longer two, but one."

One Saturday evening I sat across the table from a man whom a friend described as a good catch. After slurping down the last drop of a root beer float, he said, "Church? Funny you should ask. I don't go to church, baby, but I'll go anywhere with you."

At that moment, I realized that courting had become a predictable sweep of frustration—painful déjà vu. "Oh, really? You don't go to church? You believe in God, don't you?" I watched the second hand on my watch move twice while he thought of the right answer. *Time's up.*

He coughed up a sliver of meat and spit it into his napkin. "Well, yes, I believe in God, but Honey, we're young. Let's focus on other things. We've got plenty of time for that." That wasn't the answer I was looking for, but it was the response I had heard over and over again.

As I watched my friends date, get engaged, and walk down the aisle, I wondered if I was destined to remain single. I think some of them were curious about me as well.

"Dwan, I want to see you wear one of these some day." My friend Angela smoothed her hands over the silky material of her wedding gown. "Face it, your knight in shining armor doesn't exist. You may have to settle, girl."

"Is a nice man dedicated to God too much to ask for?" I cinched the material a bit tighter around Angie's waist and changed the subject. "There. You look amazing!"

I thought about the single life. What would I do if I remained unmarried?

I worked as an adoption counselor for a Denver-based agency, and one of my responsibilities included interviewing prospective couples to make sure they were suitable for final adoption placement. While going through my questionnaire with Mark and Janice, I asked them a routine question. "How did you decide that you were compatible for one another?"

Mark said, "I wrote a detailed list of all the things I wanted in a wife—from how she should look to what kind of personality characteristics she should have. I prayed over the list and asked God for His will. Two months later, I attended a small group Bible study, and there she was. We dated a few months, and the rest is history. That was four years ago."

I thought about his answer throughout the day. Could it be that easy?

When I returned home, I pulled out a memo pad and stared at the blank page. *Christian, nice, sense of humor, likes children . . .* Other attributes came to mind, but I couldn't decide which were vital or desirable. And I didn't want to be too picky.

On the Fourth of July weekend, I went to visit my grandparents in Tulsa, Oklahoma. I marveled at how Granddaddy treated Grandmother like a queen, even after forty years. He often brought home dinner so she wouldn't have to cook. "My feisty, little Indian girl doesn't much like to cook," he said.

During a quiet moment, I asked my grandmother a question. "How did you know that Granddaddy was the one for you? What qualities were you looking for in a husband?" My grandmother giggled like a high-school girl. Her love for her man never grew old.

When she stopped laughing, she shared a wealth of wisdom. "Well, I wanted a man who would treat me like gold—someone good with money and a hard worker; a homebody, not a run-around carouser."

After listening to my grandmother, I revised my list, adding: *frugal, likes sports, knows a lot about the Bible, educated, hardworking, compassionate, outgoing.* Without wasting another day chasing possible husbands, I diligently prayed over my list.

Two weeks later, my friend Anita invited me to church on a Wednesday night. The teacher posed several questions to the audience, many of which were answered by a man at the back of the auditorium. I was surprised by his deep, thoughtful, and wise responses to some very biblical questions. Because I was sitting at the front of the room, I couldn't see him as he spoke, but I felt strangely attracted to his calm, confident demeanor as he read scripture relating to our lesson.

I think Anita noticed my rapt attention to the voice in the back of the classroom. "Let me introduce you to Thomas, the young man who answered many of the questions tonight." She pointed me in the right direction. "He's the one wearing the turquoise Izod shirt."

My eyes immediately fastened onto a pair of enormous biceps suspended form a snug-fitting Izod. I bit my lip as I gazed at Thomas's muscular neck and wide, firm shoulders. *Could it be—muscles, Bible-wise, handsome, and a churchgoer?*

Anita walked over to fetch him, but another friend pulled her aside to talk. Because my friend Anita is long-winded, I feared Thomas might be gone by the time she finished gabbing. I had to move quickly. I weaved through rows of seats, ducked between groups of people talking, and nonchalantly positioned myself at his side.

He turned to face me.

"Hi. I'm Thomas Reed. What's your name?" The ease of our ensuing conversation left me feeling as if we had met before. Before the evening ended, Thomas asked me out on a date, and I accepted. One date led to another, and then another.

One evening, I remembered *the list* tucked safely away in my desk drawer. Thomas had every quality except one—tall. I decided it didn't matter. I could live happily ever after with someone of average height.

Besides, he towered above every man I had ever met in all the ways that mattered.

Eighteen years later, I still fall on my knees thanking God for answering my prayers in the form of Thomas—my beloved husband.

And Jesus, replying, said to them, Have faith in God (constantly).
(Mark 11:22 AMP)

—Dwan Reed

JUST ONE FRIEND

His normally cheerful face turned serious. Leaning forward and locking me in a stern gaze, he said forcefully, "I do not want to have this same conversation again in three months' time!"

He had a good point. I didn't want to have the same conversation again, either.

Looking back now, I can't remember whether it was the second or third time we had sat in that same restaurant with me whining about my predicament, and my uncle patiently—or not so patiently, in this case—doling out advice.

My problem was simple. I was a twenty-one-year-old believer in England trying to live for Christ, but finding it incredibly difficult. I had no Christian friends my age to help me stay faithful to my beliefs. Ours was a small church, and there was a twenty-plus-year age gap between me and the next youngest member.

I was hurting. The struggle felt too great to cope with alone. How could I focus on God and stand up for Him in the workplace and among my friends if I had no one to stand with me? Who could I lean on, talk to, and be encouraged by?

The older members of our congregation tried to impart wisdom and support, but I felt they were out of touch with my world. They just didn't seem to understand.

Going home after dinner that night, I prayed God would send me one friend—just one person—I could share this walk with. Surely that wasn't too much to ask.

It was 1997, and the Internet was still in its fledgling days. The difference between the online experience from then to now is incredible. Back then, the most popular Internet features were message boards and some rudimentary instant-message chatting.

I had failed to find friends in the real world, so, spurred on by my uncle's forceful advice, I sought out new ways to find the relationships I so desperately needed.

The Internet beckoned.

I started to leave messages on a multitude of Christian message boards. The difficulty was always finding the boards again the next day to see if anyone had responded. Occasionally, I would try to start new discussions of my own, but most of the time I simply responded to what other people posted.

I owned a house, but I didn't have my own computer, so my evenings were spent back at my parents' house, shut in the office and slowly trawling the web. Everything online was slow in those days. I made a few acquaintances but no real friends—and my prayers continued. Please God, just one good friend.

I don't remember the exact date I started looking for friends online; it didn't occur to me to think about that when I started, but I know it was only a few weeks into my search that April 17th rolled around. I was sitting in my parents' office for my nightly trawl of the message boards when that little voice, now immortalized in film, alerted me from the computer, "You've got mail."

I still get excited by new e-mail, even though I get dozens a day, and that day was no exception. I quickly clicked to check my mail, and there waiting for me was one new piece of unread answer to prayer, although I didn't know it at the time.

A young woman named Debbie, who was 5,000 miles away in California, had read one of my message board posts and thought I sounded sarcastic. For some reason, she thought that was a good thing and decided to contact me to say hi.

So began a game of e-mail tag. I found myself rushing home from work each day to see if she had responded to my latest correspondence and see whether or not she was online to chat. We were building a friendship. A real friendship with another Christian! It was wonderful.

What's more, not only was she a Christian, she was funny too. I hadn't even asked God for that! I didn't care if the friend I was asking for had no sense of humor at all, I just wanted a friend. But God knew exactly what I needed and provided it in a way that I couldn't imagine.

Only two or three weeks after that first e-mail, I picked up the phone to make my first phone call to the first Christian friend I had had in many years. I was very nervous. The voice on the other end of the phone sounded just the way I felt.

That phone call was the first of many, and soon we started talking every day. God had answered my prayer, and I was incredibly happy. But He wasn't done yet.

Three months after that fateful conversation with my uncle, an old school friend and I were heading off to California for a vacation and to meet Debbie.

By that time, Debbie and I were deeply in love and had to promise ourselves that we wouldn't impulsively get married while I was there.

The vacation yielded an engagement, which, in turn, brought a wedding just six weeks later.

In total, it was four months and six days from Debbie's first e-mail to the time I was watching her walk down the aisle looking more beautiful than I had imagined.

God heard my prayer for a friend and answered it with not only a friend but also a wife—a strong, loving, godly spouse to stand beside me through life's triumphs and failures, struggles and joys.

He who finds a wife finds what is good and receives favor from the Lord.

(Proverbs 18:22)

—Peter Pollock

A Dream Is a Wish Your Heart Makes

In 1978 I was eighteen, and I had never gone on a date, let alone had a boyfriend. No, I wasn't weird looking, but it seemed as though God had glued a large "Do Not Disturb" sign to my forehead to keep members of the opposite sex away.

My days started with a long commute to the Fashion Institute of Design and Merchandising; but chances of meeting a normal, nice Christian male on the public bus were dismal, at best. So every day I spent my hour-long commute nagging the Lord about wanting to go on a date.

On one particular day, I think the Lord had enough of my *kvetching*. While skimming through my Bible, the following scripture captured my attention. I could almost hear the Holy Spirit yelling the words of Psalm 37:4 at me: "Delight yourself in the LORD and he will give you the desires of your heart." At the same time, a still, small voice in my head told me to chronicle the story that would portray my wishes being fulfilled.

I went home that day, uncovered my Smith Corona typewriter, and began typing away. The title of my book was *Jesus, Wave-walker; Jesus, Joy-giver*. I placed myself in the story as the main character and described how the Lord called me on the phone to take me out on a date. And during that date, He introduced me to the man He had chosen for me.

At this point, I will digress and tell you that the name of my future husband—whoever he was—was always Michael. Whenever I referred to him in prayer or conversation, I always called him by that name— Michael. I had a list of desired attributes in my future mate: Christian, funny, handsome (to me), from a large family, nice friends, good work ethic, responsible, trustworthy, kind, handy, guitar player, and—oh, yes—he had kept himself pure for his future wife—me. Whenever I shared that last one, my friends just shook their heads and whispered, "Good luck!"

Fast-forward four years. I was attending the college and career church retreat in hopes of meeting a Christian man, though I had to admit, my hopes were waning. *Why even bother, Lord? Obviously You've chosen the single life for me.* I resigned myself to the fact that I would die an old maid. But I scanned the retreat dining room once more—just to be sure the Lord hadn't changed His mind—when I saw a face that caught my attention. I remember thinking, *He's so handsome, but he's probably stuck-up.*

I watched him meander my way. We exchanged smiles, and he sat down next to me. *May as well be friendly.* "Hi," I said. "My name is Marlayne."

"I'm Michael." Now *that* caught my attention. We chatted over breakfast then said our goodbyes. But our paths crossed many times during the retreat. We talked about our lives as single Christians, our first loves, and the fact that I was a Messianic Jew. I shared a tender story with him about how my first, albeit unrequited love, Barry, had passed away. On and on we talked, until the stars came out and we were expected back by our respective cabin mates.

Snow fell that April weekend, and when we weren't huddled in conversation over coffee, we exhausted ourselves with snowball fights. At one point, Michael caught me in his arms and kissed my forehead. I thought the snow would melt under my feet.

The last day of the retreat arrived, and Michael had not asked for my phone number yet. We would be going our separate ways shortly. So after the Sunday service, I asked to see his Bible. Pen in hand, I opened it and clearly wrote my name and phone number inside the front cover and handed it back to him. I reasoned I'd rather come off as forward than die a spinster.

The following day, I told my roommate about meeting Michael. "He's the one. I tell you, he is the one. Wait until you meet him. He may not know it yet, but I do. He *is* the one."

"How do you know?"

"I just do. That's all." I grabbed my sweater from the chair and wrapped it around my shoulders. "I'm going to visit Barry's parents. If Michael calls, call me at their house, okay?" I scrawled the number on a stray scrap of paper and pressed it into her hand. She agreed.

To my delight, while I was having dinner with Ruth and Al, she called and sang out, "Michael caaaalled!" I wanted to call him back immediately but distinctly felt the Lord instruct me to wait. I obeyed—in agony.

The next day, I returned Michael's call, and in a very nonchalant voice said, "Hi. I heard you called yesterday." Inside I was bursting with excitement. *Calm down, Marlayne.*

"Hi." His voice cracked just a bit. "I was wondering if you'd like to go see the rerelease of *Fantasia* with me. My sister Debbie, her husband, and another couple are going, and I'm in need of a date."

My face barely contained my smile. "I'd love to."

When I opened the door of my apartment the following Saturday and saw Michael standing there, I couldn't help but think, *Oh my, is he ever handsome!*

After the movie, we all went to Hamburger Hamlet for dinner. I didn't know until several years later that a very unusual conversation took place while I was in the ladies' room. Debbie's friend had asked her, "What do you think of Marlayne?"

"She seems nice," had been Debbie's polite response.

"Well, it's a good thing, because she's Michael's future wife," Tina informed everyone.

Michael was instantly incensed. According to Debbie, he exhibited an exact opposite reaction. "I'm not planning to marry anyone anytime soon. Do you hear me? No one."

Yet, nine months later Michael and I were still dating. I finally mustered the courage to show him *the story*. All I can say is, it was a good thing I waited until he realized he was *hooked* or he would have hightailed it for the hills.

Five years later, we were married. I put my story on display at our reception for all our friends and family to read how God had brought us together—and haven't seen it since. It simply disappeared.

Keep on asking and it will be given you; keep on seeking and you will find; keep on knocking [reverently] and [the door] will be opened to you.

(Matthew 7:7 AMP)

—*Marlayne Giron*

THE UNANSWERED LETTERS

Mother was moving. I'd been able to visit her once a month from another city, but now she would be living too far away for frequent visits—some seven hours away. I'd been writing her in between visits, but responses became fewer and fewer because of the progression of her Alzheimer's.

Mother loved the dignity and personal attention of receiving a bona fide letter in the mail, which made me resolve to keep writing her even though she couldn't reply.

But what would I say and send to my precious, eighty-four-year-old mom in more frequent but one-way letters? I longed for my letters to minister as much as possible, as my visits did. I importuned God to give me ideas.

His answers came gently and in timely fashion and led me to keep things sweet and simple. Initially, I felt as if I was speaking a monologue, as if I were talking to someone in a coma. Were my letters futile? Soon, I loosened up and wrote with abandon. At her new residence with my sister and her husband, Mother's superb care included Suzanne's reading my twice-a-week letters to her.

My simple letters were short—usually one page, since her attention span was compromised. I would share a particular day's activity for my husband and me. "Mel relished the oatmeal cookies I baked." Questions and jeremiads were omitted.

Seeing a sublime picture of a sunset in a magazine, I sent it. Receiving a postcard made from the photo of a grandchild excited her. When a picture didn't turn out well, I wrote something silly on the back.

Having a good sense of humor, Mother enjoyed the anecdotes and cartoons she received. She took great pleasure in the custom-made crossword puzzle with its focus having to do with things that happened long ago in her personal life.

For interest, I enclosed a flaming oak leaf, a blue-satin bookmark, a church bulletin, and once some pre-cut slips of paper to make a chain.

Sometimes correspondence was a "remember when." I would reminisce about Easters when she made dresses for us, and the to-die-for potato salad she made.

I loved to tell her of God's goodness to me. Sometimes I shared physical blessings; at other times, material ones. Since Mother was a people person, I liked to share how a friend had encouraged me.

God's inspiration and creative influence helped me turn a difficult time into one I will always cherish. He answered my prayer.

I have been young and now am old; yet have I not seen the righteous forsaken, nor his seed begging bread.

(Psalm 37:25 KJV)

—*Sherrie Murphree*

WHY DOESN'T HE ANSWER?

God, why won't You heal Jesse? I clenched my fists tightly. Hardly a striking pose in the middle of worship—and the scowl on my face? Abominable! What a contrast to the exuberant congregation surrounding me. *Do any of these people have problems, Lord? Or is it just me?*

I didn't even wait for a response. I sank deeper into my misery, and honestly, I couldn't have cared less except for that nudge I felt in my spirit. *I suppose I'd better deal with this attitude.* I closed my eyes and shifted my focus to another time, a time when this particular alive and worshiping congregation was nearly silenced. Only thirty members out of three hundred remained at that time.

"Jesse, you can't stay here. Go find another place to worship. You need a church where you can hear a solid biblical message, where you can find more fellowship. You need people, faithful people who will pray for you and your health issues."

Instead, he and two elderly members of the church met every Wednesday night for prayer. They didn't pray for their own needs, but for the needs of their congregation's remnant of thirty. They prayed faithfully for church revival, a godly pastor to lead them, and for the fellowship's financial needs.

I visited several of those prayer times, and many times felt tempted to tell the three to *get real*. As I saw it, the church was dying. But I couldn't bring myself to say it. I knew their response would be, "Only trust, Yulia."

Time passed without any visible change in the church, yet Jesse and his prayer partners never gave up. They continued praying and believing. I added my prayers to theirs, but with little expectation. Mostly I was there for Jesse. We were dating, and anything of importance to him was important to me, even if I couldn't comprehend the kind of faith that kept him believing when the circumstances remained the same—hopeless. At least that's how it looked through my eyes.

Jesse and I eventually married and moved away. Time passed quickly.

One New Year's, we decided to revisit our courting years, which included a visit to our old church. To my surprise—and Jesse's delight—the church hadn't died. Moreover, we found it was alive and thriving. A chill ran up and down my spine. I looked at my husband; he had been so faithful to pray even when it looked as though the church would have to close its doors. "God answered your prayers, didn't He?"

Jesse, struggling to balance himself with his walker, smiled at me. "He did, and He does."

"But He still hasn't healed you." I felt the frustration creeping back in.

"Yet," he replied.

The church was filled with new and different faces; we didn't recognize any of them. But the Spirit of the Living God was there, and we knew Him. One of the members approached my husband. "You're new here, aren't you? What's your name?"

"Jesse."

"Is this your first time here?"

Jesse smiled. "It's been a long time."

In that moment, I realized that God's answer might not always be what we want, or it may be delayed. Sometimes it takes years to see the answer. But He always answers. My clenched fists released by my sides. A smile replaced the scowl. My voice joined in the chorus of worship as I recalled the words of John 11:40. Jesus spoke these words to Martha before raising her brother, Lazarus, from the dead. "Did I not tell you that if you believed, you would see the glory of God?"

I looked at my husband. Grateful praise poured from his lips Even though Jesse still struggles with his health, he doesn't doubt prayer. He never did. His old church is alive and well in Florida. Jesse believed then, and he believes now. And so do I. A church that was dead is alive again.

I am the Lord, the God of all mankind. Is anything too hard for me?

(Jeremiah 32:27)

—*Yulia Bagwell*

PRAYER NUGGET

In today's culture, patience is something we need. But the process to acquire it is the miserable part. Be encouraged. Things are not at a standstill. God is busy behind the scenes in ways we cannot see. We must trust His love for us.

Lord, help me to trust You while You work things out in my life, knowing Your love for me is not in question. In Jesus' name I pray. Amen

_____

_____

_____

_____

_____

_____

_____

_____

_____

_____

_____

_____

_____

_____

_____

_____

_____

_____

_____

_____

_____

Chapter 8

RELAX! I'VE GOT IT COVERED

~ꝏ◎

A House in "Almost Heaven"

AS MY MOTHER grew older, I wanted to move closer to her in case she needed me, but it wasn't possible. I lived across the Atlantic with two special-needs children on a small farm—and no money for such a move.

When she died suddenly, her inheritance provided the means to return if I wanted to, though my reason for going was gone. Still, I felt somehow that she'd want me to come home, and when the check arrived from the estate's settlement, I went.

I had three weeks to look at houses in West Virginia. Not a lot of time. With my limited budget, many houses proved disappointing. So my real estate agent asked me to look at one that had been home to a childhood friend of his. "No," I said, when I saw the listing, "I don't like ranches, and this one looks ugly, rundown, and has poison ivy in the hedge."

"It's a good house," he replied. "Keep your options open. Just take a look."

In the end, I looked, and I had to admit it was the best value for the money—a livable, slightly shabby, two-bedroom house well within my budget. On our second viewing, the agent chatted with the next-door neighbor, a friend of his, while I began second-guessing my decision to buy any house at all. Especially when it would stand empty and neglected until we could move.

"Don't worry about that," the neighbor said. "I'll keep an eye on it for you." His name was Mike, and for some reason I believed him. He was friendly, down-to-earth, and meanwhile, I'd come to trust and love my real estate agent. Any friend of his was okay in my book. Later that day I put in an offer, and we scheduled closing for the day before I planned to leave.

We drove to the house for a final walk-through on closing day. When we arrived, we found Mike outside his own house. The windows were boarded up, the walls around them stained black: it had burned to a shell from an electrical fault the day before. His family had survived, but his dogs hadn't, and everything he owned was gone: family photos, a lifetime's music collection, all their furniture, years of memories. Everything.

I joined them just in time to hear Mike say, "The worst thing is that we're homeless. We're living in a motel." His wife had recently suffered an illness and surgery, and he worried about her after the shock of this tragedy. He looked shattered and lost.

"You'll stay in mine," I heard someone say. They turned to look at me before I realized I'd said it. I hadn't thought about it yet, but once spoken aloud, it seemed obvious. I needed someone to watch my house, and now he needed a place to live. Why not?

Over the past few days I had prayed for the house to stay safe while I was gone from it. I'm sure Mike's prayers for his family had been far more powerful than mine. I found myself wondering if my choices of towns or time to visit or real estate agent had really been my choices after all. Perhaps every step I'd taken had been guided for us, to answer prayers we hadn't even yet made.

I remembered on the flight home that Mother Theresa had once described herself as "a tiny bit of pencil" for God to write what He wished. I suddenly understood what a very great honor and joy it could be to become for just one moment a tiny, lucky bit of pencil.

Months later, I returned with my family to find Mike's house rebuilt and our own now offering a surprise: while equipping his own house with appliances and furniture, Mike and his family and friends had made sure there was enough for us too, saving us thousands of dollars and weeks of shopping. I'd never felt so grateful or so blessed, and that feeling only becomes stronger with our growing friendship.

Ranches still aren't my favorite, and I admit I still long for the big front porches or spacious attics of the other houses I'd viewed on my first visit. But my family loves this one, and no other house in West Virginia could possibly have come with such good friends as these.

> In the same way, the Spirit helps us in our weakness. We do not know what we ought to pray for, but the Spirit himself intercedes for us.
> (Romans 8:26)

—*Susan Carlton*

A NEST OF OPPORTUNITIES

"For the LORD gives wisdom, and from his mouth come knowledge and understanding" (Proverbs 2:6). I hugged my daughter, still clad in her wedding gown, with a fierceness only a mother could understand. "Don't cry, Mom. It isn't forever," she whispered against my throat. I clung to her words like a promise from Scripture.

After my only offspring moved to the other side of the country, our visits took place infrequently due to cost and distance. Friends asked me about my empty nest and how I was dealing with it. "Not a problem." I brushed them off with a laugh. "They plan to move back to Florida in a few years."

Shelly and Scott loved the beaches, the sun, and the opportunities the area offered. Soon, they would be involved in our lives again and the four of us would grow even closer. Until then, I enjoyed my writing and my time with my husband. What I didn't expect was the phone call a year and a half later.

I wanted to get an early start on the day, so I was out the door before nine. Minutes into my drive, Shelly called. Since she lived three time zones away, I was surprised to hear from her so early. I pulled over into the grocery store parking lot and hurried to answer my cell phone. Her faint cry punched the wind out of my chest. "I'm pregnant! I wish you were here."

I'm not sure what words of comfort I offered, but they certainly weren't enough to soothe either of us. That evening, I threw myself on my bed and cried out to God. *How could You do this to me? You know I always wanted to be with her when she had a baby.* My daughter's life had changed drastically, along with mine. I was certain now she would never move back. Grief clung to me like the moss on the oak tree shading our front lawn.

My life plans died that day. Everything I dreamed about changed with one call. I would miss Shelly's pregnancy, and I would be the "B" grandparent—the one the grandchild only hears about but whose hugs are rarely felt. How dare God shatter all my dreams! Shelly was my best friend. Despite the sun and warm weather, I resented living in Florida and the life I lived.

"What can I do? Do you want me to quit my job and move?" My dear husband offered what I considered the only solution for contentment. The very next morning, I soared way ahead of God—not caring what plans He had for my life. I checked job sites and moving costs and prepared to pack our belongings and sell the house. Somehow, I was certain God would make a way for us to relocate near our daughter—or at least to the same time zone. I was willing to do anything to guarantee my dream of grandparenthood.

A few weeks later, on a short visit to our home state, we enjoyed dinner with some old friends. I shared my grief with them over lost dreams. Patti reached for a book on her desk and held it out to me.

"I'm doing a Bible study about living God's will for my life." She flipped through the workbook then looked into my eyes. "You might want to do it too, and see what God's plans are for you now." Patti's married daughter and family lived nearby. I looked away. "It might help," she added.

I purchased a copy at the local Christian bookstore the next day and agreed to read it. When we returned home, I pulled the Bible study out of my suitcase and onto my lap. *Lord,* I prayed, *if You have a bigger, better plan for me out there, please show me.* My heart was broken. The grief I should have experienced months before now knocked me over with the force of a hurricane. Despite a good husband and a prospering career, I glimpsed before me a life of emptiness.

The very first chapter directed me to yield my desires to God and let Him have the final say in whatever direction I took in my life. Whoa! What was God asking of me? Turn my life over to Him? Hadn't I done that already when I became a Christian? But still, the reality that my daughter wasn't moving back remained. How would I ever be happy again?

"If any of you lacks wisdom, he should ask God, who gives generously to all without finding fault, and it will be given to him" (James 1:5). I highlighted that verse. God was asking me to trust Him, to follow His journey rather than the one I had hastily put together. Page by page, I found myself giving my life back to God—for a while—just to see. After all, the headhunters weren't knocking down our door to hire my husband, and we weren't visiting an area closer to my daughter for another month. As the days turned into weeks, I noticed little changes occurring in my life. No longer did I wake at night and brood about the sudden shift in direction God was taking me. Still, I needed something more to be content living apart from my only family. Thankfully, God heard my plea.

One Sunday morning after sitting amidst a thousand strangers in our church service, I turned to my husband. "Maybe we should change churches," I suggested. Our church was located a half-hour from our home. Despite our best efforts, we had been unable to develop a circle of close friends.

"We could always check out the small one around the corner," he said. The change scared me. We loved our pastor and Sunday school teacher, but my daughter's leaving had left an empty hole in my life, and I needed to fill it.

A few Sundays later, a woman in our new church approached me. "Would you like to come to a woman's fellowship I host every two weeks?" I could have hugged her on the spot. "I live in your development," she added. I was shocked that for the past six years we had lived down the street from each other and never met before then. I hurried home to write in my workbook how God had blessed me that day.

My journey toward contentment still involved another leg of the trip—dealing with the hazards of my occupation. I spent my days alone, writing and talking online with writers, but I enjoyed little face-to-face contact with others in my profession. Seeing an article about a new writer's group at the local library, I took a deep breath and showed up at the next meeting.

"Let me take your story home and look it over," Donna offered. To my surprise, after several e-mails, I discovered she was a Christian who had been praying as well for a friend in the community. My joy knew no bounds when we learned we once attended the same large church and knew some of the same people. Who could have planned that coincidence but God?

I still experience occasional pangs of sadness from living so far from my daughter and her family, but I trust the Lord's direction in my life. Each day, He reveals to me how His plan is better than the one I tried to create. Perhaps tomorrow His itinerary for my life will include a move nearer my daughter, but not without Him as the pilot.

But godliness with contentment is great gain.

(1 Timothy 6:6 KJV)

—Terri Tiffany

HANDLED WITH CARE

In the summer of 1990 we got a call from our friend, Craig, a field pastor ministering in a semi-remote area about five hours north of our home. "Listen, I'm scheduled to teach at a Bible camp next month, and my family is coming along as campers. I was wondering if you guys would like to housesit for us that week and feed the dog."

Vacation in the heart of lake country? That was an easy yes! Excited about this opportunity, we asked his permission to invite two other families from our church to join us. Craig's large country home offered plenty of room for our combined group of six adults and six children.

The area boasted numerous beautiful lakes for swimming, boating, fishing, and lots of hiking trails. We spent several sunny days participating in a variety of recreational activities. Evenings were occupied playing board games, reading, and enjoying each other's company. We were having a great time and things were going smoothly until early one midweek afternoon when the front doorknob fell off. We had noticed it was wobbly, suffering the combined effects of age and wear, and definitely not repairable. But where could we find a replacement for something so old and unique?

The house could not be left without a lockable front door. If anything, our desire would be to leave the place in better condition than we found it. In our concern, the group of us, both young and old, joined together to pray for guidance and a solution.

Although it seemed highly unlikely that a new doorknob would work, we decided we must try to find a replacement. One of the guys in our group, John, had an engineering background and thought perhaps he could devise a way to adapt something to fit. While two adults remained behind with the kids, four of us piled into our car and headed into town to check out the local hardware store.

About three miles down the highway, we spotted one of those perennial yard sale signs. "Hey," I said, "let's stop and take a look."

"Oh, okay," my husband replied, and turned into the long, dirt driveway. On one of the tables we noticed a box of doorknobs and rummaged through it to no avail.

Then one of the fellows casually asked the vendor, "You wouldn't happen to have any more door handles kicking around, would you?"

"I think I might," he replied and marched off to a nearby shed. He returned moments later with a small box of assorted hardware. "Take a look through here and see if you can find what you're looking for," he offered. Imagine our total amazement when we sorted through that odd collection of discards to find the exact doorknob we needed. It looked to be in perfect working order and cost us the grand total of one dollar!

"This is unbelievable!" I said. Equally amazed, everyone agreed. We hurried back to the house to share the good news with the others. They were just as excited as we were. It was a wonderful lesson on the power of prayer, not only for the children but also for us adults, as well as a reminder of God's provision and faithfulness.

Often we think that we shouldn't bother God with what seems like an insignificant issue, and we neglect to come to Him in prayer for such things. This experience taught us that God is concerned about even the small problems we face, and He has a "handle" on everything.

For nothing is impossible with God.

(Luke 1:37)

—*Sheila Wipperman*

THE WHITE, BABY GRAND PIANO

I will never forget the Sunday morning when our pastor taught on this verse. "Delight yourself in the LORD, and He will give you the desires of your heart" (Psalm 34:7).

Delight in His ways; delight in His Word, delight in praise and worship to Him, delight in Him. The pastor said, "As you delight in Him, He is the one who gives you the desires that come into your heart. The more you delight in Him, the stronger the desire becomes." It kept going over and over in my mind, and as I meditated on it for several days, it finally took root in my spirit.

I noticed as I hungered more after righteousness, as I delighted more in Him and in His Word, the more passionate the desire to have a baby grand piano grew in me. Both my husband and I played the piano, and my daughter and son were taking piano lessons. I saw a real gift in both of my children, and I wanted that gift to grow. I prayed that the Lord would somehow allow us to purchase a baby grand piano.

I began looking at pianos and pricing every brand out there. The piano I wanted was going to run into a great deal more money than my small salary could accommodate. I looked at brown ones and black ones and white ones. I looked at $20,000.00 pianos and at $400.00 pianos.

I listened to their tonal qualities and began to pray more specifically, *Lord, You said if I would delight in You that You would give me the desires of my heart. Lord, I desire a white baby grand Yamaha piano. I cannot afford $20,000.00, but I know with You nothing is impossible.* I patiently waited to see how God would answer my prayer.

I was a master barber and had a young woman apprenticing under me. She had heard me talking about the piano for six weeks. One Monday morning, Karen bolted into the salon clutching a piece of paper.

"Kandy! You've got to see this," she said. "You'll never guess what is in my church bulletin."

A broad smile spread across my face as I read, "Baby grand piano for sale." I called the phone number in the ad to schedule an appointment to look at it, and a short time later my husband and I were pulling into the seller's driveway.

He asked, "Are you the folks who called about the piano?"

"Yes, we are."

As the owner opened the front door, I saw a beautiful, white, baby grand piano. I sat down to play. The touch was incredible, the tone astonishing. Further examination revealed it was a Yamaha. Then came the question. *What was the price?*

The owner said, "We purchased the piano six months ago for $16,000.00." They were reluctant to sell, but his company was transferring him and his family to California. They needed to sell it before they moved. "We'll sell it for $4,000.00."

"That's still a great deal of money for us. I will have to pray and get back with you," I said.

On the way to the car my heart was excited and sick at the same time. It was exactly what I had asked the Lord for, and the price was amazing. Roger looked at me and said, "Do you want that piano?"

I knew in my heart that was my piano and that God had answered my prayer, but I was hesitant because I wasn't sure I could make the payments. Roger asked me again, "Do you want that piano?"

I checked my heart and said, "Yes."

He said, "At that price, you'd better not wait. It will be sold." So we returned to tell the family we would take the piano. With God, all things are possible. And with His help, I paid it off in eighteen months. It seemed like a breeze. There was so much beautiful music that came from a precious desire that came from God. My children are grown and gone from home, but every time I look at that beautiful white piano, I thank the Lord for His sweet goodness and blessing in my life.

If you, then, though you are evil, know how to give good gifts to your children, how much more will your Father in heaven give good gifts to those who ask him!

(Matthew 7:11)

—*Kandy Sharp*

GOD'S PROVISION FOR A RUSSIAN GIRL

During a tennis tournament in the summer of 2001, a fifteen-year-old world-ranked Russian player and her coach stayed in our home in Lexington, Kentucky. The first morning before breakfast I said to my guests, "We are Christians and always give thanks for our food before we eat."

You could almost see the question mark on Nina's face. She understood some English. Praying was definitely not a part of her life experience.

The great commission tells us in Mark 16:15 and Matthew 28:19 to go into the entire world and preach and teach. In this particular account "the world" had come to me. In fact, I was hostess to these two from Russia, where I have never set foot.

As the week progressed, the Lord gave me a real love for this young girl and a deep concern for her spiritual state. His Word tells us in 2 Peter 3:9, "He does not want any to perish, but everyone to come to repentance." I prayed throughout the week that I could find an effective way to communicate the gospel to Nina. I stayed alert for any opportunity that might present itself.

The 9/11 act of terrorism against the United States occurred while Nina and her coach were in our home. They expressed deep concern and interest, in spite of the language limitations, as we watched the news on television. This created more of an atmosphere of unity and friendliness. It also provided a setting that led to conversation about death and the brevity of life.

While attending a dinner party celebrating the birthday of a friend, I was recounting the story of our houseguests. I shared my concern for Nina's salvation. The hostess, Becky, asked, "Would you like the four spiritual laws salvation booklet in Russian?"

As stated earlier, I had prayed for some way to effectively witness to Nina. Becky went to her basement and returned with the Russian booklet. Wow! Talk about answered prayer!

The next day I asked the Lord to help me select a gift for Nina at the Christian bookstore. In conversation with Nina, I learned that she liked sporty jewelry. A braided stretch bracelet with metal hearts intertwined in red, gold, blue, and green strands caught my eye. The perfect gift!

Two days before she was to leave, I found Nina reading while waiting for her coach to get ready. They were off for another long day of tennis. This was the moment of opportunity I had prayed for. I went in, sat beside her on the bed, and asked if she enjoyed reading. "Yes," she replied.

I said, "I have something for you to read in your language that will tell you know how much God loves you." Her face registered surprise as I handed her the booklet in Russian. I gave her the bracelet explaining that the little silver hearts were to remind her of God's love for her and my love for her as well. Perfect timing.

As the two prepared to leave that day, Nina had tears in her eyes as we hugged each other. I have never heard from her again, but I praise the Lord that she has the simple gospel in her own language. I prayed she would be drawn to read the booklet.

> So is my word that goes out from my mouth: It will not return to me empty.
>
> (Isaiah 55:11)

—Peggy Park

PRAYER NUGGET

If we look at our own inadequacies and capabilities—things and situations may appear to be impossible. But when we bring God into the situation, the dynamics change. For what is impossible with man is possible with God. He wants us to depend on Him. Make a note of current situations you feel helpless about and commit them into His hands.

Lord Jesus, help me to remember to invite You into the impossibilities of my life. In Jesus' name I pray. Amen.

_____

_____

_____

_____

_____

_____

_____

_____

_____

_____

_____

_____

_____

_____

_____

_____

_____

_____

_____

_____

_____

_____

_____

_____

_____

_____

_____

_____

_____

_____

_____

_____

_____

_____

_____

_____

_____

_____

_____

_____

IS THERE ANYTHING
I CAN'T DO?

‑‑※‑

CHEMICAL CRASH

"NO!" I SHRIEKED. Crowded around a small wall mirror at my weekend spiritual retreat, a girl accidentally splattered my face with her hairspray. For most people this is no big deal; however, my body is chemically sensitive and reacts violently to solvents and perfumes. The symptoms take seconds to appear and two whole days to subside. Trying not to panic, I hurried to wash it off but the damage was done.

A whopping headache quickly materialized from inhaling that sprayed chemical. I became dizzy and clutched a friend's arm to keep my balance as I stumbled into a chair for our morning devotions. Sounds were muffled, my heart pounded rapidly, and a dazed feeling covered me. My numb face didn't prevent the burning inside my nose. I could see the speaker's lips moving but I couldn't hear any of her words.

I sat there helpless and in a stupor until a strong, tingling sensation began all around my neck. This prickly feeling slowly moved upward to the top of my head and disappeared, taking the numbness with it. My head cleared, my hearing returned, and my heartbeat slowed down.

Bewilderment permeated the turn of events because all the side effects of that blast of hairspray were going away. Unlike any other chemical crash I've experienced, I suddenly felt better in a very distinct way. Relieved, I gave my attention to the speaker.

Later in the day, my group visited the church's prayer room, which was filled with people. One unfamiliar lady asked all of us, "Which one of you is Cindy?" I immediately became self-conscious and wondered, *Oh no, what did I do? What's going on?* I reluctantly raised my hand, and all the eyes in that room turned toward me.

Smiling, she continued, "How are you feeling?"

I thought that was an odd question. I became intensely aware that everyone in that room was looking at me with some anticipation. "Fine," I replied hesitantly, clueless as to why I was receiving this attention. This inquiring lady proceeded to inform us that our group leader sent a note downstairs to the prayer room when she heard about and observed my condition that morning. In response to the note, one of the retreat's ministers anointed this informative woman on my behalf while everyone in the room prayed for my immediate healing. They also prayed that the incident would not interfere with my retreat.

The hair on my arms stood up. I had completely forgotten about the health problems I experienced earlier since no symptom of that crash had lingered. Recalling everything that happened to me that morning, I became deeply humbled. People whom I did not know had lifted me up in prayer before the Lord.

As I pondered these things the day after the retreat, I happened to read James 5:13-15. "Is any one of you in trouble? He should pray…Is any one of you sick? He should call the elders of the church to pray over him and anoint him with oil in the name of the Lord. And the prayer offered in faith will make the sick person well."

Stunned, I reread that passage. Those prayer chapel participants took the initiative to follow the Bible's instructions while I became the recipient of answered prayer and experienced a miraculous recovery. At the request of a group of people who believe in the power of prayer, God caused every adverse symptom to disappear from my body. I was fully healed within a couple of minutes, and it occurred as the prayer was offered for the restoration of my health.

Hurray! God not only listens and responds to His believers' prayers, He still performs miracles. I've learned that the outcome of disasters can be a joyful occasion when the Lord is asked to intervene.

Even though I walk through the valley of the shadow of death, I will fear no evil for you are with me; your rod and your staff, they comfort me.

(Psalm 23:4)

—Cindy Rooy

ROAD TRIP TO HEALING

It was the mid-sixties. Our family was in turmoil. I was in pain and desperate for answers and relief. My pastor father said, "God is here and He cares." But where was He when I contracted a crippling case of juvenile rheumatoid arthritis just before my thirteenth birthday?

I'd always been the healthiest member of the family. My younger brother and older sister contracted all the usual childhood illnesses. I got nothing—not even when I crawled into bed with my sister when she had measles. Mom's face said it all. "Carolyn, get out of here right now! I don't want you getting sick too."

I didn't. I was healthy, strong, athletic, loved the outdoors, and wanted to become a jockey before women were allowed to be jockeys.

Things changed as I reached adolescence. In just a few months I went from walking and running to being confined to a wheelchair. I couldn't even wheel myself. My legs contracted and refused to straighten, despite therapy. My fingers curled. Pain—agonizing pain—confiscated my days and danced in my nightmares. My parents argued constantly about treatment. The elders of the church prayed, and my parents wept as they bombarded heaven on my behalf. Food turned my stomach, and my weight dropped until I avoided looking at the skeleton in the mirror. Family, friends, and strangers prayed. Thoughts of suicide poked their way into my mind. A way out? Perhaps, except my parents had laid too good a foundation.

I knew God was real. I knew He'd died for me and had risen for me. I knew, despite the horror of my present situation, He had a plan and a purpose for my life.

God, what are You doing? I cried. Fear twisted my insides. Would things ever change? Would I be forever locked in this struggle where even the simplest movement brought excruciating agony? Medication helped, but only a bit.

I sensed the deep pain in my father when he announced he planned to drive me to Texas, fifteen hours away, where a revival conference was taking place. He'd run out of ideas, run out of solutions, and run out of anything but laying his daughter's needs before the Lord.

Bundling me up, he laid me gently on the back seat and made sure I was as comfortable as possible. From the car window I watched the sun rise in the sky, and the air grew warm as we traveled south. At times we talked, and at times I slept. I sensed prayer was never far from my father's heart.

Traveling was a strain on me. It made me stiff and sore if I didn't get relief at regular intervals. Every couple of hours we stopped. Dad would haul out the heavy wheelchair and lift me into it, and we would enter some restaurant for a quick snack or meal and move on. About 4 P.M., Dad found an inexpensive motel and checked us in for the night.

Because my dad was a pastor, we lived modestly, and the trip to Texas was a hit on our family's finances. Still, Dad said, "This is what I feel God wants me to do." The next day we reached our destination and found the motel Dad had booked for the week of the revival conference. Day after day we sat in the auditorium and listened to preachers preach the Word and watched others go forward and many get healed.

At night I went to bed, exhausted and still hurting. The week drew to a close, and Dad's frustration and impatience was evident. I saw him waylay one of the ministers, who had no answers for him. "After all, it is God who heals, not man," we were told over and over during the week.

The final night Dad took me down front for prayer. I felt fear and hope and embarrassment as I waited my turn with the rather flamboyant man who ministered that night. I'd seen him around all week but had no idea he'd taken note of me until Dad pushed my wheelchair in front of him.

He searched my face. "I've been praying for you all week," he said. A chill zipped up my spine. Would this be my moment? I bowed my head when he placed a cool hand on my forehead and began to pray. I have no idea what he said. The auditorium, the preacher, everything faded away as something began to happen. I felt—saw—a huge key entering a lock, and suddenly a thousand doors, one after the other, sprang open. The prisoner was set free. I felt it, felt something change inside. For the first time in years, my pain was gone!

I told the preacher, "It's gone. The pain is gone." He tried to have me stand, but my limbs hadn't changed. My fingers remained gnarled, my knees were still permanently bent, but inside I was free. God healed me where I most needed it, inside. I left smiling.

Dad was bitterly disappointed. He wanted his little girl to be whole. Back at the motel, I got ready and slipped into bed. My father—never a big proponent of pills—tried to get me to take my pain medication. I shook my head. "Dad, I really don't need it." I saw the struggle on his face, but he let it go.

The next morning we headed home. Much to Dad's amazement, not only did I sit up most of the way home, but we also made the return trip in one long drive. No frequent stops and no overnight stay. And no pain meds.

We had left home praying for healing. My family never realized I needed healing inside much more than outside. God brings hope and healing in His way, in His time. With the pain gone, I was able to work at straightening and strengthening my arms and legs. It was a struggle.

Years later, after college, I entered the hospital for six weeks of joint replacements and reconstructive surgery. It took a year, but I relearned how to walk. In that year, I found my soul mate, Keith, and I walked down the aisle without my wheelchair—without braces or crutches—to stand with my groom before my misty-eyed father as he pronounced us man and wife.

> And we know that all things work together for good to them that love God, to them who are the called according to his purpose.
>
> (Romans 8:28 KJV)

—Carolyn R. Scheides

MIRACLES STILL HAPPEN

In this modern world of science, miracles still happen. Jesus is with us today, just as He was with His people two thousand years ago. One night Jesus touched me and a miracle happened.

At the time, I belonged to a prayer group that met every week to praise the Lord, sing, and pray. I had recently been baptized in the spirit. As a busy young engineer, besides my projects, I traveled for my company and tried to faithfully attend these prayer meetings. They gave me renewed strength to face the world.

I wanted both my soul and body to remain healthy, so I had a complete physical once a year. When the time arrived for my physical, my wife told me to show the doctor a mole on my back.

During my annual physical, I showed it to our family doctor. "I don't think it's anything," he said. "But you should see a dermatologist to confirm that it's okay."

I made an appointment with the dermatologist, but since our family doctor didn't seem concerned, I wasn't in a hurry. After I showed the dermatologist the mole, he grunted and said, "It's a little suspicious, but I don't think it's anything. I'll cut it out and send it in for analysis. Come back in three weeks."

In the next three weeks of my busy schedule, I didn't think much about it except that the incision didn't heal. I remember the day I walked into the doctor's office—it was a beautiful, sunny, spring day, but the words the doctor spoke chilled the air. When he entered the examining room, I said, "Doc, it hasn't healed."

He looked at his chart, grunted, mumbled to himself, and then said, "No wonder! It's cancer. I'll try to cut it all out. If it doesn't heal in three weeks, that means I haven't gotten it, and we'll have to go on from there."

That evening, I attended the prayer meeting and told the group what the doctor had said. Their response was to pray for healing. They laid hands on me and prayed that Jesus would heal my back. I accepted the healing and thanked Jesus.

Three weeks later I attended another prayer meeting, and the group asked me about my back. I told them that it still hadn't healed.

Someone said, "Let's pray again for healing," and they all agreed.

I said, "No. Why pray again? I've already accepted the healing."

That night, we sang and praised the Lord, and I felt uplifted and ready to face the world again. While driving home that night, all of a sudden, I felt as if a hand touched my back. A wondrous power flowed into my body. It was a wonderful, glorious feeling. I can't even start to describe it. Even though I was driving, I let go of the wheel, lifted my hands and praised the Lord.

When I got ready for bed that night, I pulled my undershirt off, and a scab fell on the floor. I felt my back and looked in the mirror. There was nothing—not even a scar. The doctor couldn't explain it, but I could.

Praise the Lord, O my soul, and forget not all his benefits—who heals all your diseases.

(Psalm 103:2-3)

—Leon Arceneaux

NOTHING IS TOO SMALL

"Honey, we need to talk." My husband, Tom, had just met with our field leadership in Brazil, where we served as missionaries. As we sat in our living room at the mission base, Tom shared the details of their conversation. "Considering the decrease in our financial support, it's necessary for us to begin home ministry sooner than anticipated. Hopefully, we can raise the needed support and be back to Brazil in a year. But with a number of supporters out of work due to the recession, it will be a challenge. Arrangements are being made for you and the girls to leave next week, but I will need to stay another two weeks until Sylvia returns from Germany to take over in the office."

The news came as a shock. I was saddened at the thought of leaving our dear Brazilian friends and mission colleagues on such short notice. But I knew God would meet our financial needs; we had learned to trust Him with big challenges. At the moment, I had to focus on making preparations for our flight home.

It was a very hot, humid day. Many of our friends found the climate stifling, but I didn't mind, since I feel the cold easily. When making a list of what to take home, I realized I would need a sweater for the plane. We didn't need sweaters in Brazil, and I didn't know where I would find a sweater in the tropics on such short notice.

As I headed downtown, my prayer was simply, *Please, Lord, let there be a sweater somewhere.* I couldn't think of anywhere I had ever seen sweaters for sale. I began walking down all the usual streets to no avail. Turning left off what we called the "walking street," I went three blocks and turned right.

I spotted a store with a sign that read "Clothing for Travel to the South." Since Brazil is south of the equator, travelling south means going into a cooler climate. Would I find a sweater in that store? Perhaps!

I walked into the shop and asked the man behind the counter if he had any sweaters.

"I do, but I have only one," he replied.

I asked to see it, and it was perfect and just my size. And on sale! Needless to say, I bought it, and I left the shop with a very thankful heart.

I still have that sweater, and the paper it was wrapped in. They serve as reminders of the faithfulness of our God! He is God of the details, and nothing is too small for Him. If it matters to us, it matters to Him!

On the flight from Brazil to Miami, that sweater kept me cozy. After we arrived at the Miami airport and were preparing to leave for our hotel, we discovered there were no hotel rooms available in all of Miami—even for those who had confirmed reservations. Hurricane Andrew had torn through Miami the week before, leaving countless people homeless. All hotels were housing those who had lost their homes. Even the airport was filled with homeless people. And it was so cold! The Lord knew I would need that sweater not only for the flight but also for that very cold night in the airport.

Cast all your anxiety on him, because he cares for you.

(I Peter 5:7)

—Lynn McCallum

THE COURSE THAT ALMOST CONQUERED ME

Anatomy and Physiology—the most difficult college course ever. No matter how hard I studied, I couldn't master the coursework, and I ended the semester with a barely passing grade. I decided to retake the class during the summer to improve my grade. I figured without other classes to distract me, I would have a much easier time with the material.

Wrong! That summer I spent night and day doing little else but studying, yet it still didn't seem to be enough. Once again, I was three chapters behind in my reading.

One morning, stressed and worn out from a night of cramming, I stumbled through my morning routine. As I backed my car out of the driveway, I crashed into my parents' garbage cans. *Figures!* And the morning didn't get better. When I arrived at the university, I accidentally hit my chin on the car door, causing tears to well up in my eyes. I was exhausted, weak, and my chin hurt, but my class—Anatomy and Physiology—was calling me.

After class, I went to the university's student center to catch up on more studying, but pure exhaustion overcame my will to concentrate. *I should never have taken this class again. I'm just not smart enough.* I struggled to keep from sobbing.

Not knowing what else to do, I prayed quietly. *God, I need strength—Your strength. I can't make it through this class, or any classes, without You. I could really use a hug from You too.* As I continued praying, the outside of my lips started to turn upward. I felt so much joy that I laughed out loud. People around me probably wondered if I'd finally cracked under the pressure of my studies. But I didn't care.

I was shocked at the sudden shift of my feelings. Weary sorrow had turned to joy. I remembered Nehemiah 8:10: "Do not grieve, for the joy of the LORD is your strength." God was filling me with His joy. I attacked my reading with gusto and finished all three chapters. The joy and renewed sense of strength lasted throughout that semester, and when grades posted, I walked away from the board with a smile—and an A!

Give me a sign of your goodness, that my enemies may see it and be put to shame, for you, O Lord, have helped me and comforted me.
(Psalm 86:17)

—*Angela Banks*

MY KUNG FU BATTLE

Screeching tires startled me to the core. An oncoming car fishtailed as the driver frantically sought to control his vehicle to avoid hitting mine. *Well, Lord. You missed me that time. Try again.*

I had become a Christian only months before that bizarre prayer. Eager to learn as much as I could about God's will, I had attended as many Bible studies and church meetings as possible since surrendering my life to the Lord.

During one meeting, the pastor preached on the extraordinary obedience of Isaiah and Ezekiel. Isaiah, at God's command, walked around town for three years—naked. And Ezekiel, commanded by God, had to lie on his side for months at a time. He ended his message by issuing a challenge, "If there is anything in your life that hinders your obedience to the Lord, I invite you to surrender it to Him now."

I thought of my dedication to martial arts training. I never missed a workout. My instructor recognized my resolute commitment and, as a reward, offered me a key to the studio to let myself in for early workouts. He called on me to lead the class in exercises, and before long I was selected, along with an elite group of others, for secret training. My goal was to break bricks and boards with the back of my hand. I was deeply immersed and even more determined in my training and objectives.

But I wondered how God felt about my desires as a Kung Fu expert. *Lord,* I prayed, *I give You permission to remove all things, including martial arts, if it's not in Your plan for my life. I cannot take myself out of it because I love it so much. But Father, if You take it away, please pull it out by the roots so I won't go hungering after it again.*

Over the next few months, I thought the only way I would leave Kung Fu is if I suffered some sort of accident that would prevent me from participating. It was the only thing I could think of that would make me give it up. Mistakenly, I believed the near-accident was an unsuccessful try by God to make that happen, so I prayed that He would try again.

I continued my Kung Fu training. However, I noticed that rather than working out with my usual enthusiasm, I found myself pacing the workout room. "Vanity of vanities; all is vanity." I repeated this portion of Scripture from Ecclesiastes 1:2 (KJV) over and over with every step.

My workouts became forced out of discipline rather than driven with the fervent passion I was accustomed to.

A few weeks later, the instructor announced that I would be testing for advancement to black belt. My skills were vastly improved, and I was able to backhand smash against stone lampposts without pain. I had also fearlessly battled an opponent much larger than myself in a recent tournament. However, I didn't quite feel ready to advance to black-belt level after training for just under a year. Even though I felt honored to be elected for promotion, I sensed my advancement was premature.

When the day of testing arrived, I had doubts that my performance surpassed the quality needed to advance. Yet to my surprise, the teacher stiffly awarded me the highly coveted black-belt sash. I could tell he was less than pleased with my execution, and I wondered why he would promote me to this level.

And then, a fleeting thought crossed my mind. *He wants a black belt student in his class for marketing purposes.* At that realization, I left the class and never went back.

I realized that the Lord had reserved an option I would never have considered to remove a deep-seeded obsession from my life. Brute force, the only option I believed would have ripped me away from the *idol* of my life—martial arts—was not a part of God's plan. Instead, He did exactly as I had prayed. He completely removed the root of my desire to pursue further advancement in Kung Fu. And in time, I gathered all the martial arts books I owned and tossed them into a dumpster. I turned in all of my weapons to a bewildered police officer at the local station.

Prayer from that point became open-ended from my perception. No longer did I venture to guess how the Lord would accomplish His will, only that He would. And in each instance, He exceeds my wildest expectations.

He brought me forth also into a large place; he delivered me, because he delighted in me.

(Psalm 18:19 KJV)

—*Steve Husting*

PRAYER NUGGET

Cynicism can grow around our hearts like the hardened skin of an alligator. We lose that simple ability to believe and hope that we had when we were younger. Jesus teaches us to come to Him as if we are little children. That hasn't changed. We just forget.

Lord Jesus, please remind me to come to You as a little child, bringing my requests, trusting You with my cares, and simply believing the promises in Your Word. In Jesus' name I pray. Amen.

_____

_____

_____

_____

_____

_____

_____

_____

_____

_____

_____

_____

_____

_____

_____

_____

_____

_____

_____

Chapter 10

FROM A TO Z

⤜✲◯

ORDERED STEPS

STRANDED MOTORISTS ARE a common sight along the Houston freeway system. Any time I see someone in this predicament, I pray for him or her.

As a woman traveling alone, I don't stop to render aid. I'm certain God knows about the situation. He knows the specific needs and also who is available to be of help. My part is to pray. I pray for the strangers' safety and for God's provision.

One afternoon, I was on my way to seminary class and decided to stop for a latte. I exited the freeway and drove along the feeder road toward the intersection where I would make a right turn. When I approached the intersection, I saw a young woman with an apprehensive look on her face sitting alone in an old red truck. It was stopped and blocking the flow of traffic. In order to make my right turn, I had to go around her.

Helpless to move the pick-up, I watched as frustrated people jeered at her. Passing her as I made my turn, I whispered, *Lord, please send someone to help her. Surround her with Your peace until help arrives.* I continued on my way to the coffee shop.

Usually after purchasing coffee at this shop, I continue on to class on the back streets. I rarely return to the freeway since there are various merging roadways nearby and it's difficult to maneuver the interchanges. But this day, I returned the way I came. Approaching the feeder road, my heart rejoiced at the scene before me—the woman's truck was being pushed across the intersection toward safety.

When the two trucks passed before me, I looked into the face of the young woman I'd prayed for. Our eyes connected, just for a moment. How I longed to say, "God made a way for you." Instead, I settled for communication through my face and hands. With a smile as big as Dallas, I raised my hands and clapped to demonstrate my joy for her good fortune, followed by a big thumbs-up.

God ordered my steps that day to meet two needs: for the lady in the truck and for me. I needed to see His activity alive in my world that day, maybe more than the lady in the truck did. The experience uplifted and encouraged my heart, and I wanted to shout.

The steps of a man are established by the Lord; And He delights in his way.

(Psalm 37:23 NASB)

—*Anita Onarecker*

THE PRAYER THAT CHANGED MY PRAYERS

With an armload of towels, I headed to the linen closet, opened the door, and leaned my head against the sheets inside. I sobbed, *Oh, Lord, teach me to pray; if You never teach me another thing, teach me to pray.* I knew God wanted me to pray, but I still struggled every day trying to communicate with Him. I realized the problem did not originate with God; it originated with me.

Before that day my prayers seemed so lifeless and dull. I would say *Bless my family, I love You, praise the Lord,* and then struggle to find the words to pray. I would read a Psalm, ask God to bless Aunt Susie, and then struggled again, quickly running out of things to say. I did not realize it that morning, but my relationship with God was about to change.

After putting the towels in the closet, I walked to the kitchen table and looked out on the backyard. God had outdone Himself this spring. The back yard was filled with pink roses, lavender and blue hydrangeas, and bright-yellow lilies, all sparkling in the morning sun. Earlier, an azure haze covered the garden but slowly gave way to the warmth of the sun as the birds began to sing.

I sat at the kitchen table and looked through the bay window at the array of multicolored flowers and thought, *God how creative You are. This garden is only the smallest reflection of Your glory.* I began to praise the Lord spontaneously for His beautiful creation in my backyard. My prayers grew more joyful as the time ticked by. I thought of all the marvelous things God had done in my life, how He planted me in a good place, even though at times I struggled to raise my head up from the miry clay.

He taught me many lessons from the garden as I praised Him for the times He had watered my soul with the water of His Word when I was dry. So often He lifted me up when I felt weak and ready to wilt, like a flower suffering from drought. I asked the Lord to prune me when I needed it, even if it hurt and I looked awkward for a season. I knew God's pruning would cause new growth and spiritual maturity. Prayer time flew by, and before I knew it an hour passed.

That morning Jesus met me at my kitchen table as I praised Him for the beauty of His magnificent creation and went on to praise Him for His goodness in my life. God directed me how to pray, and His presence was like a warm blanket comforting me.

Now I look forward to my prayer time. I write in a prayer journal, dating each entry, so I can go back and write down the dates when the answers come. God directs me to the Scriptures and teaches me how to pray them back to Him in my own words. The Scriptures have become my personal prayer book, and I never run out of words.

Not in my wildest imaginings did I think one simple prayer could change my entire relationship with God. As I leaned into the linen closet that day, God heard my prayer, and I know it pleased Him.

Being confident of this very thing, that he which hath begun a good work in you will perform it until the day of Jesus Christ.
(Philippians 1:6 KJV)

—Marty Prudhomme

LIFE VIGIL

Trust in God. Be silent and simply observe what is going on around you. Often questioning life's happenstance yields no answers, and attempting to bulldoze through problems creates more anxiety.

This quiet observation is a life-lesson I was destined to experience again and again. Most of the teaching moments in my life came through illness—both mine and my patients. The graces of simplicity, patience, and prayer, along with quiet observation, got me through many dark nights. Of all life's wonderful virtues, quiet observation can reveal precious moments that may otherwise be missed. One such moment changed my life forever.

Ella asked, "Will you participate in the death vigil for Linda?" This request stemmed from the knowledge of my previous work in hospice and hospital care of the terminally ill. Ella's request posed a special circumstance, however. I had met Linda, her best friend, a year before. She had the progressive, terminal form of multiple sclerosis. Since I live with multiple sclerosis, that diagnosis hit very close to home. It was important that my attendance at Linda's life transition not overwhelm the patient or me.

"Ella, I need Linda's approval first," I said.

Linda welcomed me graciously to the final moments of her life. This blessing would stay with me forever. She had decided on a 24-hour vigil as soon as the doctor had deemed her time on earth was coming to a close. Four-to-eight-hour shifts were established with friends and acquaintances to ensure that Linda would not die alone. She wanted people close by that shared her strong spiritual belief in God and the afterlife and would see her moving on as something to be celebrated rather than a morose departure. I fit her criteria.

Later, I realized it was Ella, our mutual friend, who needed my support more than Linda did. Linda, now in her final moments of life, was the victim of tragic circumstances. Years ago, she was a clumsy teenager who married at age twenty. Life as a newlywed was rosy until the birth of her daughter. Then the clumsiness escalated until she became wheelchair-bound. It was only after she crashed physically that it was medically determined that she had multiple sclerosis. The results of her diagnosis were neither pity nor empowering support, but rather abandonment. Her husband not only left her but also emptied the bank account. Family was nearby but unwilling to assist with Linda or her baby. After a year of trying to care for herself and her daughter, she realized her handicap might endanger her child. She could no longer care for herself or her baby.

With profound reluctance, at twenty-three years of age, Linda entered a geriatric facility. Her child was placed for adoption. My friend Ella had worked at that same nursing home twenty-five years ago when Linda entered. Close in age, they had struck up a friendship that included long chats and outings. They had remained close since that time.

Now Linda, in her fifties, was dying. Ella and I entered Linda's private room at the nursing home only to find her comatose. Ella, normally stoic and strong, began to cry. Her reaction tugged at my heart. The person from the prior shift informed us that Linda has been comatose for the last eight hours.

"We're too late," said Ella. "Oh, Linda! I'm so sorry we're late."

I attempted to console her by telling her that Linda knew on some level that we were there and that she would be able to hear mental talk and prayers, but Ella didn't respond. She was devastated. Ella sat by Linda's bedside, took her hand, and sobbed. There was a chair at the back of the small room, and with the assistance of my Lofstrand crutches, I made my way to the chair. Our vigil began.

Over the years I have found harp music to be extremely comforting during MS attacks. While my mind and body heals, therapeutic music soothes the erratic neurological firings in my brain. Cognitive impairment—the confusion, mental fog, and loss of clarity that accompany MS attacks—seems to be eased by a harp's mellow strings. Anxiety and pain are reduced. Listening to harp music allows me to float away gently into a kinder, less harsh existence. So I placed my recorder on the floor beside me and turned on the tranquil CD that I carefully selected just for Linda. It is music for life transition. I recited a few prayers and concentrated on the scene before me. *Linda, wake up,* I said silently. *Just for a few minutes. Your best friend, Ella, is here and needs you. Please acknowledge her. It will just take a minute; then you can rest in peace.*

The hours dragged on, and the nurses came and went. They decided to withhold all medications, as Linda was no longer responsive. Years ago, as an RN in hospice, I had made similar decisions. As my MS progressed, though, physical nursing work became difficult. Soon, I didn't trust myself to make some medical decisions. Leaving nursing devastated me. Soon, canes, crutches, and wheelchairs became my legs. Music calmed my frazzled nervous system. Volunteer work like this filled my soul once more.

It had been a while since I worked hospice, but this vigil was familiar. While with a dying patient, I often mentally told him or her that it was okay to let go; there was no need to hang on, and a new life awaited her. My plea this time, however, was unique. *Wake up Linda, only for a moment.*

Ella got up to stretch and walk around. I took her position at Linda's bedside. Linda's mouth was open and her tongue dry. I found some lemon glycerin swabs in her bedside table and began to swab her mouth. I gently placed her drooping head back into alignment while whispering to wake up.

A strand of gray hair fell onto Linda's face. I gently brushed it in place. Her shut eyes squeezed and then relaxed.

"Our relief is here," Ella said quietly. "It's time to go. Oh, Linda, I wish you would wake up!"

I patted Linda's hand one last time and prepared to move so that my friend could say her goodbyes. Suddenly, Linda's head turned toward me. She opened her eyes and said, "How are you?"

It's odd for someone to recover so spontaneously from a coma, but not unheard of. I paused for a moment, thinking she didn't know me, but her steady gaze was convincing. Linda knew me very well indeed.

I smiled down to the suddenly lucid patient. How could she remember me? We had met only once, more than a year earlier. Then I wondered. Had she had heard my mental pleas? I quickly dismissed this thought and remembered Ella. "Someone has been waiting for you," I said and then moved away. Ella had a very private, brief chat with Linda.

Soon, the patient looked at me again and whispered, "The struggle is worth it." Tears sprung to my eyes. Linda had suffered in many ways the past two decades. Her plight had been much more severe than mine.

But Linda seemed to glimpse a rich, spiritual destiny and a swift end to her suffering.

"Smile down on me," I whispered back. "I accept all help." Linda closed her eyes for the final time.

My faith tells me there is a very full and abundant afterlife. I believe to the core of my being that the mysteries of the Father, Jesus Christ, and the Holy Spirit will be revealed when we transition to our next life. The joyful contentment, the graceful inner stirrings felt during lifetime on earth will multiply in heaven.

For me, stillness is the thread that joins a spiritual life with physical existence. *Quiet observation* may open a soul to ethereal understanding in life. With this knowing lies peace. And all your troubles in this life, all the struggles and hardships, will have been worth it.

Be still and know that I am God.

(Psalm 46:10)

—*Diana Amadeo*

New Steps of Faith

With a black, clunky, special-made orthopedic shoe on my right foot and a black sock stretched over my knee-to-ankle-length cast on my left leg, I wobbled into Dr. Peek's office. The smile I wore revealed not only joy, but also all thirty-two of my bright, white teeth!

I had quit using my crutches a few months earlier. These days I couldn't quit smiling. Maybe because I truly appreciated life since a truck ran over me, breaking 111 long bones. In addition, the accident also damaged my heart valves. But I'm alive!

I turned toward the gentleman next to me and said, "Thanks for getting the door."

"Sure," he said, but his baffled expression said volumes as he gave me the once-over. At age twenty-three, I had experienced many such encounters. I had grown accustomed to stares that read, *How could a person like you, with all those bright pink scars, be so happy?* One person actually said, "If I were you, I'd wear jeans and a long-sleeved shirt!"

I didn't take her advice. Our sunny California weather called for shorts and tank tops, so that's what I wore. I did start wearing a sock over my cast when I noticed an elderly man glance down at my foot where the cast ended. Seeing that my toes had been amputated, he looked me straight in the eyes and sneered in disgust. In haste, I turned my head so that he wouldn't see the tears filling my eyes.

As I waited to see Dr. Peek, I prayed that my body was strong enough for the cumbersome cast to be permanently removed. I had a special reason. I would be going on my first church retreat in the Big Bear mountain area of San Bernardino, and snow was in the forecast.

"Vanessa," Dr. Peek's assistant called out, "you're next." She directed me to the room, where I positioned myself on the cushioned table. Following the removal of the cast, Dr. Peek entered. His eyebrows furrowed as he examined my scrawny, bare leg.

"The tibia is osteoporotic so we have to put the cast back on." He continued, "I'll order a bone stimulator and call you as soon as it comes in. Hopefully, it will promote the hardening the tibia needs."

I smiled and said, "It's okay, Dr. Peek. This afternoon my friend from church is picking me up for a weekend retreat up in Big Bear. We'll pray that God will heal it."

Unenthusiastic, he mumbled, "Okay, I'll pray for you too."

That weekend, even though I had to hold on to friends to avoid slipping on the ice, I relished the beauty of the snow and the mountainous sights around me. I focused on Jesus and sang praise and worship songs to Him. *And* asked Him to harden my tibia.

The following Wednesday I returned to Dr. Peek's office to receive the new bone stimulator. Sitting on the same cushioned seat in the same room, after the cast removal, Dr. Peek and I stared in awe and amazement. This time, the bone was strong and stationary—osteoporotic free!

With a smile from ear-to-ear, Dr. Peek said, "We'll leave the cast off."

While the Lord hardened my bone, He softened my heart, making it flexible and open to trust Him in all ways.

… For I am the Lord that healeth the.

(Exodus 15:26b KJV)

—Vanessa Ingold

FLAT TIRES

I jumped backwards as a freight truck flew by and clipped the mirror on our SUV. My husband, Scott, raked his hand through beads of perspiration. "Where is God when you need Him?"

He slung the flat tire to the shoulder of the road, put the spare on our camper, and began to turn the lug bolts. The sun, hot enough to fry a turkey in peanut oil, boiled us. Finally, we climbed back into the Chevy Suburban and continued our journey through Tennessee, grateful for the air conditioning that blew in our faces. In Gatlinburg, we parked our travel trailer at the foot of a mountain. Weary from our travels, sleep came early.

The next morning as we headed to another campground, rubber started flying, and the trailer began to vibrate with another flat. I held my breath and silently prayed as Scott stood on the side of the road and changed another tire. He unhitched the Coachman from the SUV, and the tongue jack broke. This time he had to get between the Suburban and the camper with eighteen-wheelers flying past, whipping wind in our faces. If another vehicle hit the back of the travel trailer, he'd be pinned and smashed between it and our SUV.

"This time we don't even have a spare." He unhitched our American Coachman and left it on the side of the road while we drove several miles to find a tire. He explained to the repairman that it was our family vacation, our second flat, and we'd left the travel trailer on the side of the interstate.

God bless that man. That's the quickest I've ever seen anyone replace a blowout. We returned and found the camper safe, and Scott put on the new tire so we could head to the last campground we planned to visit.

Miles later, rubber began spiraling through the air, and I heard the thump, thump, thump of another flat. Scott pulled over in front of the office to the campground, our next destination. He drove to the campsite and unhitched the camper. "Hop in. We've got to locate a spare tire."

In the middle of the woods, with nothing on the side of the road but trees for company, we followed the ribbon of two-lane blacktop that curved like a black snake winding its way through a maze. Finally, we came to a small town and found a gas station. "I doubt they'll have camper tires," he said.

The manager said, "You're in luck today. We've got one that size, and there's nothing else for miles around."

"I'll take it." He brought the tire back to the site and put it on the trailer. "I hope we don't have more flats. There are no tires."

Back at the campground, we enjoyed the woods, river, and swimming pool, and we relaxed after our stressful road trip. "When we aren't on the road dealing with flats, it's peaceful. I never thought I'd get to see such sights." I smiled at him, reached over, and stroked his hand. "Tennessee is beautiful."

"You're not the one who has to change all the flats." He grinned. "I've never had so many at one time. Those camper tires have to be defective."

"I'm still enjoying the sights and the trip."

The next morning, we pulled over for gas before we continued our trip home. Back on the interstate, a few miles down, we came across a horrific accident in which an SUV and a camper trailer had overturned. "That could have been us, especially with all those flats," Scott said.

"And you wondered where God was when you needed Him. He's been with us every mile of the way." I smiled, looked heavenward, and said, *Thank You for a vacation of answered prayers.*

A righteous man may have many troubles, but the Lord delivers him from them all.

(Psalm 34:19)

—Barbara Russell Robinson

OUR SON IS MISSING

It was December, and my family had traveled to Duncan, Oklahoma, to visit my dad for Christmas. The day before we were to return to our home in Spring, Texas, we had a nightmarish scare.

I was in the family room that day when Dad came in. He said, "I'm going over to Tracy's (my sister-in-law) to try to fix her water leak."

"Okay. What time do you think you will be back?"

"I don't know, but I'll take Morgan with me," he said, indicating my nephew. About ten minutes later, the doorbell rang. I got up to answer it and glanced over at my ten-year-old son, Timothy, who was watching a movie on television.

When I opened the front door, my mouth dropped open. Looking up at me with his big brown eyes stood our eight-year-old son, Joshua, with the dog, Angel.

"What are you doing out here? And how did you get locked out?" Questions rolled out of my mouth.

"Grandpa asked me to bring Angel in," Joshua said.

I asked him again, "But how did you get locked outside?"

"I don't know," he answered.

"All right, come back inside and play." I locked both the deadbolt and the lock on the knob of the door. As I turned around, I noticed Timothy watching me. I didn't think anything of it at the time, and I gave him a quick hug and left the room.

I walked into the family room to chat with my husband, Joel, about some things we needed to do. "Timothy's been trying to wear his jogging pants all day," said Joel. "He's been putting his shoes on too."

"What did you do?"

"I finally hid the shoes and kept telling him we're not going anywhere," he said. "I know it's fifty-five degrees, but it's still too cool for them to play outside."

"Hold your thoughts," I said as I left the room, "I'll be right back."

As I paused briefly at the bathroom door, something caught my eye. The front door in the living room stood wide open. "Who unlocked the door?" I asked Joel urgently.

A quick search of the house confirmed that Timothy was nowhere to be found. His jogging pants were missing as well. Frantic, Joel put his shoes on and raced out the door after him. I grabbed the truck keys, told Joshua to keep an eye on Nathanael, and ran out the door. Tossing the keys to Joel, I ran across the street to the neighbor's house. My heart raced.

"My son is missing! Have you seen him?" I broke into tears as fear gripped my heart.

"No," she said, "but let me ask my husband." She hurried back into her house.

"Paul, this woman's son is missing. Have you seen him?"

A man came to the door and said, "I saw him playing outside a few minutes ago." Handing me their phone, he said, "You need to call 911."

As I waited for the call to connect, I prayed silently. *Lord, please help us find him soon. Keep him safe.*

A woman's voice on the other end of the line said, "What is your emergency?"

"My non-verbal, autistic son, Timothy, is missing," I cried into the phone.

"What does he look like and what is he wearing?"

"I think he is wearing black jogging pants. He doesn't have shoes on, and I don't think he has on a shirt. His hair is brown."

The 911 dispatcher said, "Wait just a minute while I check our information." That minute seemed like an hour before I heard her voice again. When I did, she said, "An officer has him and will bring him to you." Then she clarified the address with me and asked my name.

Stunned, I said, "You mean he's already been found?"

"Yes. An officer will bring him to you," she repeated. My eyes darted to the street, looking for signs of an approaching police car.

Minutes later, I spotted the patrol car driving toward us. "There it is," I said to the operator. Ending the call, I handed the phone back to the neighbor. I gratefully walked toward the police car.

The officer questioned me regarding the circumstances of our situation. I said, "We are visiting my dad for Christmas. Our son, Timothy, is non-verbal autistic. He unlocked the deadbolt and left without our knowledge. We were in the back part of the house." Shifting from one foot to the other, my anxiety mounted. About that time, another police car turned onto the street. I started toward the approaching car to get my son.

"He's not in there," the officer said. I stopped, dejected. The other officer got out and walked in our direction.

"Your son is fine. He was found in the middle of Highway 81. Our officers had trouble catching him. He kept running from us." I gasped in horror at the thought of what could have happened.

"He's autistic," I explained, tears streaming down my face.

The officer spoke up. "We figured that was most likely the case. Another officer familiar with autism helped us catch him. You need to call us quicker the next time."

"May I use your phone to notify my husband that he's been found?" I asked. I spoke briefly to Joel and then turned back to talk to the officers. They assured me that someone would bring Timothy to us soon. When the next police car came into view, I waited patiently, hopeful this one had Timothy in it.

Then, the first responding officer spoke the most beautiful words this mother's ears could hear. "Go get your son." He didn't have to tell me twice. I ran to the car, grabbed Timothy, and sobbed as relief washed over me. After the officers left, Joel and I praised God for answering our prayers.

For God hath not given us the spirit of fear; but of power, and of love, and of a sound mind.

(2 Timothy 1:7 KJV)

—*Robyn Cederstrand*

My Struggle with Cigarettes

I worked away from home in Yellowstone Park—my own man—when I was eighteen years old. When my new buddies offered me a cigarette, I'd say, "Smoke chokes me."

One of the guys showed me how to inhale into my nose. That made the smoke less irritating, and I decided to have a smoke once in a while. My smoking started just so I could feel that I was part of the social group. That old line, "Everybody smokes!" helped make it seem reasonable. So an offered cigarette was taken with the thought that *a few can't hurt.* What self-deception that proved to be—actually a mental lie.

Ever so gradually, one became two and two grew into a habit imbedded in my brain. It wasn't long before I bought my first pack. Holding my habit to one pack a day became a difficult challenge. *I can quit any time I want to,* used to be true, but the kick in the pants for me was always starting again. I would quit for forty days every year at Easter time. Twice in my life the Lord helped me quit for longer periods, but I'd tell myself, *Just one won't hurt.* The addiction crept back, and I'd be hooked again.

I smoked from the age of eighteen to age sixty. Every year into my fifties I had been able to quit without too much difficulty. After that, when I tried to stop smoking, I was Mr. Miserable—and hard to live with.

On May 1, 1993, I awoke and said, *Jesus, I want to give up smoking, and I need Your help.* In that instant, all desire and need for nicotine left me. From that moment forward I have never had another cigarette—or the desire for another one. To me, knowing my past history, this is a miracle.

Since that moment, being around people who are smoking doesn't bother me, and I'm not tempted. Any time the subject of smoking comes up, I say, "I used to smoke, but I quit May 1, 1993. I didn't quit by myself. Jesus took away all desire so I didn't have any struggle at all." Then I tell them of my prayer and the miraculous answer I received.

When suffering the grief of my wife's death to cancer, I was tempted to start smoking again. Fortunately, the voice of faith and reason merged, reminding me that God helped me quit three times, and it isn't wise to smoke and later ask for help to stop again.

> They cried unto thee and were delivered; they trusted in thee, and were not confounded.
>
> (Psalm 22:5 KJV)

—Edward Reinagel

NOT GUILTY

Capital murder—how could this happen? It was 2003, and my best friend, Austin, was arrested—on Mother's Day weekend. He was thirteen years old. Along with his half-sister, they were both charged in the shooting death of his half-sister's ex-husband.

Mom told me the news, but I just couldn't believe it. I denied it for a long time. In my heart, I felt I might never see him again. That motivated me to pray almost every minute of every day for his situation.

Although I believed he was innocent, how could I be sure? A few days later, he called from the jail and we had a lengthy discussion. I listened as he told me what had happened. In my grief for him, tears filled my eyes and dripped off my chin.

"Natalie, please, you've got to believe me. I did not pull the trigger," Austin said.

I believed him. "That's all I wanted to hear, Austin."

From that day on, I trusted his version of the shooting and was confident he would be set free.

But that was not in God's plan, at least not then. Austin was tried, convicted, and sentenced to life in prison with no chance of parole until he was seventy-five. I couldn't believe it! Why was God doing this? What reasons could He have for keeping him in jail?

This bazaar turn in Austin's situation made no sense, but my faith was strong. My first act every morning was to pray for Austin's release. It was also the last thing I did before going to sleep at night. But somehow I knew God had a reason behind this delay.

With Austin in jail, I was at home—missing my best friend. His daily phone calls began to take their toll on our finances. And like many struggling families, the costs soon mounted up and the calls came to a screeching halt.

We continued to communicate through letters. I received a letter from Austin almost weekly, and I wrote faithfully to him from June 2003 until June 2008.

In spite of the bleak situation, my friends and I continued to trust God. We knew He was in control. And Austin's faith never wavered. He also knew that God would take care of him, no matter what or where.

Five years later, in 2008, Austin was granted a new trial. It had been a few weeks since I had received his last letter. In it he had written, "Pray that God will overturn the conviction, and I will come home." And pray I did.

Every day I watched for word of his trial on television or in the newspapers. I prayed and waited for any shred of news. Two weeks later, Austin was granted a new trial, and the jury found him not guilty. Not guilty!

What a blessing to my heart it was when I read the wonderful news. I leaped for joy! The newspaper quoted Austin's tearful response, "I just thank God that they saw the truth. Thank God!"

He was set free. With God *all* things are possible—even the impossible.

Austin is now in college, studying to be a paramedic. God is working in his life every day and helping him achieve his dream. He has been out of jail for more than a year now, and has so much to be thankful for.

God has His own timetable, and this was His for Austin. I learned the great power of prayer.

Therefore I tell you, whatever you ask for in prayer, believe that you
have received it, and it will be yours.

(Mark 11:24)

—*Natalie White*

PRAYER NUGGET

No matter what the issue you're coping with, God is acutely aware of it. He is omnipresent, omniscient, and all-powerful. Difficult for our minds to comprehend, but His Word is full of rich examples of His greatness. If you have not asked Him to forgive you your sins and invited Him into your heart as Lord and Savior, don't put it off.

Lord Jesus, please forgive me of my sins, wash me clean with Your blood. Come into my heart and make me a new creature. Fill me with Your Holy Spirit. In Jesus' name I pray. Amen.

_____

_____

_____

_____

_____

_____

_____

_____

_____

_____

_____

_____

_____

_____

_____

_____

_____

ABOUT THE CONTRIBUTORS

Diana Amadeo is an award-winning author who has publishing credits in books, anthologies, magazines, and newsprint; most notably *Chicken Soup for the Soul, Pauline Books and Media*, Zondervan, *Guideposts*, and *Boston Globe*.

Yulia Bagwell is originally from Ukraine. By God's grace, she received her bachelor's degree in Belarus and a master's degree in America. She and her husband, Jesse, live in Philadelphia, Pennsylvania.

Angela Banks is originally from Cincinnati, Ohio. She is currently a graduate student in counseling psychology at Ball State University. In her free time, she loves to read, write, volunteer, and spend time with friends and family.

Leon Arceneaux is the published author of five books, an award-winning short-story writer, and a world traveler. He is a retired engineer, ordained deacon, and serves as chaplain at a local hospital. He and his wife, Marjorie, live in The Woodlands, Texas.

Esther M. Bailey is a freelance writer who has a passion to share the good news of Jesus Christ. She lives in Scottsdale, Arizona, and attends McDowell Mountain Community Church.

Grace Booth is a retired teacher and freelance writer. Her articles have been published in many magazines and book compilations. She lives with her husband, Doug, in Picayune, Mississippi.

Renie Burghardt is a freelance writer who was born in Hungary and came to the United States in 1951. She is published in seventy books, magazines, and online venues.

Denise Chang is a wife, mom, teacher, and dedicated traveler. One of her greatest joys is connecting kids to the world around them. She and her family live in Castle Rock, Colorado.

Susan Carleton blogs daily at <www.stonyriver.ie>. Her fiction and articles have appeared in print and online. In 2008, she received the Bursary Award in Literature from the Arts Council of Ireland.

Robyn Cederstand is a stay-at-home mother of three autistic boys. She enjoys reading, writing, cross-stitching, and hanging out with her family. She and her husband have been happily married for fifteen years.

Sally Clark writes from her home in Fredericksburg, Texas. Her work has appeared in *Indeed, Relief: A Quarterly Christian Expression Journal* and *Purpose*, as well as numerous anthologies. Visit her web site at <www.sallyclark/info>.

Jan Cline is a freelance writer, author, and singer from Spokane, Washington. She writes a column for <WAHMZone.com> under the Family Zone section. Visit her at <www.jancline.net>.

Andrew Culbertson is a freelance writer and member of the final graduating class of Taylor University Fort Wayne. He enjoys reading, running, and mission work around the globe.

Lisa Plowman Dolensky is mom to three miracles and also a Pre-K teacher. Her stories appear in *Chicken Soup for the Soul: A Book of Miracles* and *What I Learned from the Dog*. She's a University of Alabama Longleaf Fellow and a <www.newpages.com> reviewer.

Elsa Dotson is a writer, teacher, and conference presenter. Recognized by President Reagan as a Volunteer Candidate of the Year, she and her husband have traveled extensively throughout the world. They now reside in The Woodlands, Texas.

Debra Elliott is a Christian wife, mother, grandmother, and author. *Life Through the Rearview Mirror* is her first published book of poetry. She is a contributing author in *Heavenly Humor for the Cat Lover's Soul*.

Marilyn E. Freeman lives in Florida with her husband, Bruce. She has two daughters, ten grandchildren, and one great-grandson. She has been published in several magazines. She is the author of two children's books, *Summer Adventures with Grandma* and *Pasquale's Journey*.

Twilah A. Fox, M.D. is a practicing psychiatrist for many years, a published author, and speaks on the spiritual aspects of mental health. She has found this to be a much-neglected area in her field of medicine. Married fifty-five years, she is also a grandmother.

Marlayne Giron is the author of *The Victor*, her first novel. She has been married to her husband, Michael, for twenty-three years, and they are the parents of fifteen-year-old Karina, their daughter. Marlayne is a Messianic Jew.

Sally Hanan left Ireland with her family in 1995 when she and her husband got lucky with the lottery visa. She lives in Texas and serves as a youth pastor and lay counselor in her home church. She owns a freelance editing business, <www.inksnatcher.com>, and is working on a romantic suspense novel.

Charlotte Holt, author of *Praise the Lord for Roaches!* is a freelance writer, speaker, and retired teacher. Her stories appear in *Guideposts Books* and *A Scrapbook of Christmas Firsts*. She lives with her husband, Charles, in Kingwood, Texas. Visit her at <www.charlotteholt.org>.

Connie Huddleston served for twelve years as a missionary in Panama. The maternity outfits went with her, were worn during her second pregnancy, and then shared with other missionary ladies on the field. Connie now serves as children's minister at her church in Lawrenceburg, Indiana.

Steve Husting is a mild webmaster by day and fearless writer by night. His works are regularly published in the iTunes Store and Daily Devotions for the Deaf.

Vanessa Ingold is known as "a walking miracle." At age twenty-three, she was run over by a truck while riding her bicycle, and her injuries required twenty-seven surgeries. She has been published in many book anthology articles. She lives with her husband, Greg, in Southern California. You may reach her at <JCnessa@aol.com>.

Lisa Keck is a writer, wife, and mother. She has written devotionals for <Christiandevotions.us> and is also published in print. She enjoys finding spiritual applications in everyday life.

Mimi Greenwood Knight is the mother of four who lives in South Louisiana with her husband, David, and too many pets. She enjoys baking, birding, Bible study, and the lost art of letter writing. Visit her at <blog.nola.com/faith/mimi_greenwood_knight/>.

Sherri Langton is associate editor of *Bible Advocate* magazine and *Now What?* e-zine. She's also a freelance writer and workshop speaker at writer's conferences. Sherri lives in Denver, Colorado.

Catherine Leggitt is a wife, mother, grandmother, author, and editor presently residing in northern California. During her first career—after raising children and before caring for aging parents—Catherine worked as an elementary teacher, where she developed her storytelling skills.

Mike Lynch's first two novels, *When the Sky Fell* and *American Midnight*, both published by Silver Leaf Books, came out in 2009 and 2010 respectively. Ellechor Publishing released his third novel, *After the Cross*, in 2011.

Lynn McCallum served with her husband, Tom, as missionaries in Brazil. They are now involved in church planting among immigrants and refugees. She is currently writing her first novel. Lynn and Tom reside in southern Ontario. They have two adult daughters and two grandchildren.

Janetta Messmer is an award-winning inspirational author who resides in south Texas with her husband, Ray. Her publications appear in *Guideposts Magazine, Guideposts Books,* and she was given honorable mention in *Writer's Digest Magazine.*

Sherrie Murphree is a former English teacher who loves to encourage others in writing. She also teaches a women's Bible study at her church. She resides in Odessa, Texas, and has been published in thirty different magazines and nine book compilations.

Linda O'Connell lives in St. Louis, Missouri, with her husband. Her inspirational stories appear in *Chicken Soup for the Soul* and other books and magazines. Linda is an early childhood teacher. Visit her at <www.lindaoconnell.blogsport.com>.

Rebecca Joie Oakes lives in Florida with her husband and children. She is active in Christian youth and counseling ministries.

Annette O'Hare is a Christian author and sketch writer from Porter, Texas. She and her husband of twenty-five years, Dan, are parents to Patrick, Casey, and Connor. The O'Hares are active members of First Baptist Church Porter, support the Texas A&M Aggies, and enjoy saltwater sport fishing.

Perry Perkins is a novelist, blogger, and stay-at-home dad who lives with his wife, Victoria, and their young daughter in the Pacific Northwest.

Peter Pollock is a husband, father of three, house-church pastor, stay-at-home dad, blogger, and writer. He also runs a web-hosting business and loves to get out and be Jesus' hands and feet in his community.

Marty Prudhomme is a freelance writer from Mandeville, Louisiana. She has taught and written Bible studies for twenty-five years. She is currently vice president of leadership training on the state board of Aglow International and serves as the outreach coordinator at her local church.

Dwan Reed is a licensed master of social work, and a former child therapist and school social worker. She now spends her time as a writer, inspirational speaker, real estate agent, preacher's wife, women's prison evangelist, and African missionary. Dwan can be contacted via dwanbooks.com.

Edward Reinagel is the father of ten and enjoys writing. His books, *Eight Ways to Share Your Family* and *Pump Up Your Prayer Life* can be found on Amazon. Just enter his name.

Barbara Russell Robinson lives in Florida with her husband, two dogs, and a cat. She's a graduate of Christian Writer's Guild and Long Ridge Writer's Group and the mother of five children, who have made her grandmother multiple times. Visit her at <www.barbarajrobinson. blogspot.com>.

Cindy Rooy is an inspirational columnist for two Tennessee newspapers. She is the author of a Bible study titled, *Trusting God Through Troubles & Tears,* and is a contributing author in a few devotional books. Cindy also enjoys a speaking ministry. She has three grown children, and presently lives in Kingsport, Tennessee, with her husband. Visit Cindy's website at <www.cindyrooy.com>.

Carolyn R. Scheidies is an award-winning author of more than twenty-four published books. She writes a regular column for the *Kearney Hub*, speaks to a variety of groups, and runs several web sites including <www. IDealinHope.com> and <www.IDealinHope.com/bookreviews>.

Kandy Sharp is the president and founder of Sharp Word International Ministries. She and her husband, Roger, have ministered the Word of God in love, word, and deed in more than forty countries in the past fourteen years. She is a speaker and teacher and loves people of all cultures and ethnic backgrounds. The Sharps have two children and two beautiful grandchildren.

Aggi Stevenson is an award-winning writer, CLASS communicator, a businesswoman, and Bible study leader. She is the wife of one, mother of three, and nana of nine.

Susan Sundwall is a freelance writer, children's Christian playwright, and a multi-published author. Her stories appear in *Cup of Comfort for Dog Lovers II, Guideposts: Miracles in Tough Times,* and *HCI Ultimate*

Gardner. She writes from her home in upstate New York, where she is working on her first novel.

Sue Tornai's articles have appeared in *The Lookout, The Upper Room, Light & Life*, and *Pockets*. She has worked on assignment for Standard Publishing, Augsburg Fortress, and Christian Ed Warehouse.

Danielle VanMeter writes from her home in South Africa. She enjoys reading, singing, and spending time with her four sisters. She hopes to encourage other Christians through her writing and throughout her life.

Natalie White lives in Mississippi with her parents and several cats. She enjoys writing, taking photos, selling online, creating different things and crafting. God placed in her heart a love for writing at age thirteen. Visit her at <Pioneer-Writer. blogspot.com>.

Sheila Wippermann is an award-winning author whose publishing credits include *Reader's Digest,* Warner Press, Dayspring Greetings, Andrews McMeel Publishing, and Oatmeal Studios. Her story, "A Christmas Miracle," appears in the anthology *Christmas Miracles*, published by St. Martin's Press in October 2009.

Anita Onarecker Wood authored *Divine Appointment: Our Journey to the Bridge.* She is a speaker, minister, and leader of women's ministry in Texas. Visit her web site at <www.anitaonareckerwood.com>..

Susan Kimmel Wright is the author of many articles and stories as well as three novels for teens. She is married and the mother of three adult children.

SCRIPTURE LIST

Introduction

Psalm 139:13 AMP

Chapter 1: Work Is Good for the Soul

Psalm 31:15a
Psalm 19:14
Psalm 91:14-15
Jeremiah 29:11
1 Chronicles 16:15
1 Chronicles 5:20b
Proverbs 3:5-6

Chapter 2: No Worries

Psalm 107:15
Philippians 4:19 KJV
Psalm 18:6
Luke 19:10
Psalm 32:6a
Isaiah 65:24, Psalm 32:7
Psalm 119:65 KJV

Chapter 3: Hey! I've Known You Forever

Psalm 86:10
Psalm 104:24 KJV
Psalm 105:1 KJV
Matthew 6:28-31
Psalm 139:15-16a, Joel 2:28-29
Psalm 139:14
Psalm 84:11 KJV
Psalm 139:16

Chapter 4: All in the Family

Hebrews 10:23 KJV
Proverbs 18:24a KJV
Psalm 5:3
Proverbs 13:19a
James 5:15, 2 Thessalonians 15:16-17

Chapter 5: Gifts That Keep on Giving

2 Timothy 1:7, 2 Corinthians
    12:9, Proverbs 18:10
Psalm 138:8
Psalm 91:2
2 Chronicles 16:9 KJV
3 John 3 KJV

Chapter 6: You'll Never Guess What Happened!

Psalm 23:1
Malachi 3:16-17 KJV
1 Kings 18:24
Psalm 34:15
Matthew 6:8 KJV
Matthew 7:7
Jeremiah 33:3

Chapter 7: Love Is Patient

Mark 10:8, Mark 11:22 AMP
Proverbs 18:22
Psalm 37:4, Matthew 7:7 KJV
Psalm 37:25 KJV
John 11:40, Jeremiah 32:17

Chapter 8: Relax! I've Got It Covered

Romans 8:26
Proverbs 2:6, James 1:5, 1 Timothy
    6:6 KJV
Psalm 37:4, Matthew 7:11 KJV
2 Peter 3:9, Isaiah 55:11

Chapter 9: Is There Anything I Can't Do?

James 5:13-15, Psalm 23:4
Romans 8:28 KJV
Psalm 103:2-3 KJV
1 Peter 5:7
Nehemiah 8:10, Psalm 86:17
Ecclesiastes 1:2, Psalm 18:19 KJV

Chapter 10: From A to Z

Psalm 37:23 NASB
Philippians 1:6 KJV
Psalm 46:10
Exodus 15:26b KJV
Psalm 34:19
2 Timothy 1:7 KJV
Psalm 22:5 KJV
MARK 11:24

W.

WinePressPublishing
Great Books, Defined.

To order additional copies of this book call:
1-877-421-READ (7323)
or please visit our website at
www.WinePressbooks.com

If you enjoyed this quality custom-published book,
drop by our website for more books and information.

www.winepresspublishing.com
"Your partner in custom publishing."

CPSIA information can be obtained at www.ICGtesting.com
Printed in the USA
LVOW060442230911

247526LV00001B/5/P

9 781414 119823